the articles

First Edition 2005

Printed in the United States of America on acid-free paper

ISBN 0-9764940-9-4

Published by:
Westview Publishing Co., Inc.
8120 Sawyer Brown Road, Suite 107
Nashville, Tennessee 37221
www.westviewpublishing.com

CONTENTS

"Man who chases two rabbits
has no meat for dinner"

Chinese Proverb

INTRODUCTION

Managing for Profitability

I started writing a few articles a couple of months ago to address a certain group of profit centers. This group of profit centers was challenged to make money even though they were trying as hard as they could. I started thinking about their situation and drew a couple of conclusions that led to those articles, which led to this book. My conclusions were as follows. First, there are things that can't be taught. If you can't figure out how to develop a customer relationship, then I can't help you. So I concluded that there is no need to talk about that much. Second, there are things that are taught all the time. We have all heard 38% this and $10k GP/employee that and six turns, etc. etc. So there is no need to talk about that.

Then there is the big group of things that, in my opinion, affect everything, yet don't get as much discussion time. This book is about everything that is important, but isn't often taught.

My hope is, that the reader (the target audience is a profit center manager), after comparing his/her profit center against the subjects in this book will find at least a few things that are mitigating profit, if not eliminating it. Some profit centers make a fair amount of money, and some make a lot more than that. My belief is that almost any profit center can make substantially more. I also believe that making substantially more isn't all that hard. If you are reading this and thinking, "Man, I am running the truck tires till they are bald, I am using borrowed #2 pencils to the nub, and I am working 60 hour weeks, yet I still can't make a reasonable profit", then this book is for you.

I am a firm believer that being a CED profit center manager is the best job in the world. Where else can you run your own business, and get paid part of the profits for what you did-other than if you actually did own the business? And when you reap the benefits of those successes in the form of profit sharing, you can smile knowing that it was all your doing.

Among other topics covered in this book are the importance of, and relationship between market focus, customer selection, capacity, and customer service. These subjects are covered in great detail because, though it is simple to understand the concepts, it's not easy to do. Shortcomings in these areas look like this:

- The profit center is losing money with no clear way to get profitable.
- Though the P&L shows that there are more employees than there should be, everyone seems overworked.
- Because everyone is so busy, customer service is poor. Everyone talks about "our great customer service", but it isn't really there.
- It would take more business to turn a profit, but more resources to handle the business.

- Many management decisions are very difficult for you to make.

I hope you are able to sort through the myriad of concepts (I hesitate to just describe the solution), and find a few ways to make more money for your people, and have more fun doing it.

Randy

A DAY IN AN ELECTRICAL DISTRIBUTOR MARKET

Bob is having a good day. As the manager of "The Big Contractor Pipe and Wire House" (TBCP&WH) he has always had a passion for selling the big commodities to the big contractors in town. As a part of that passion, he has always paid particular attention to the wire markets and put a lot of effort into being the dominant wire supplier in his market. Knowing that wire will go up quite a bit next week, Bob has secured pricing on three truckloads of wire below current levels with a commitment to buy a fourth truck at the same levels within a month. Of course, that is a bunch of wire, but Bob, being in the business of selling lots of wire to big contractors has called all of his favorite contractors and told each of them of the pending doom of the prices skyrocketing in the next week. He has received commitments from each of the contractors to purchase most of the wire that he is about to buy. Due to his savvy negotiating (which he can do on wire because he is in that business), he is going to make a very nice profit on four truckloads of wire. What a good day.

Joe is having a good day also. Joe runs the "Industrial MRO electrical supplies" (IMEC) distributor in the market. Joe has always known that there had to be some kind of opportunity with one of the large industrial users to whom he sells. Though Joe has a respectable position at the account there is no real purchasing strategy, which is noticeable by the fact that they buy from a number of suppliers and basically just hand orders out. Joe had been thinking about this for quite some time and finally decided to make a pitch to the head guy at the large industrial plant to enter into a single-source, strategic sourcing agreement with Joe and IMEC. Because of Joe's creativity (which he has because he's in that business) he was able to save the customer money while raising his margins through negotiations with the manufacturers, not to mention that he has now quadrupled his business at one of his largest accounts and shut the door on the competition. Now his selling job will be much easier because he won't have all those competitors nipping away at his hard work all the time. Joe is truly having a good day, oblivious to the fact that the price of wire is going up next week.

Sally is having a great day. All Sally thinks about 24 hours a day is how to get better at fixture job business. The BIG order has been on the street for a couple of weeks now and she finally snagged it. The company she runs, "Fixture Job Business Supply House" (FJBSH), is known for being the best in the market at managing a multi-hundred thousand-dollar fixture order like this one. That reputation put her in the driver's seat with both the customer and the manufacturer's, allowing her to negotiate a good order with nice margins. Unlike many other distributors, Sally is feeling pretty confident that, not only will her job management team handle the order very well, allowing her to make a nice bottom line profit, she is certain that it will serve to further strengthen her reputation and relationship with the contractor. What a great day, Sally muses as she ponders the big order of the year. Of course Sally doesn't care about copper, and doesn't know what MRO stands for.

Pat is having a different day. Pat is out making sales calls like he does on his regular routine as an outside salesman. He gets up first thing in the morning and, because it's Tuesday, he goes to his favorite high-volume contractor (which is a big deal, because he has about 20 of them). Upon arriving at 7:00 AM, he chats with the receptionist for a while and drops off the donuts for the estimators. Then Pat goes to see the owner, Charlie, with whom he has a great relationship. Feeling confident, Pat goes through the initial warm-up process and then pulls out his best pitch--"anything I can help you with today." Charlie ponders that difficult, probing question for a while and responds, "I don't think so Pat. The only thing I can think of that is going on is that we just purchased quite a bit of wire from TBCP&WH. I would have given you a shot, but you guys really can't compete with them on the commodities." Pat, not feeling too good about that conversation grabs a donut and heads to his next call.

Pat's confidence has been shaken a bit, but things are about to get better. Since it's Tuesday, his second call is to his favorite industrial, where he has done business for over a decade. The strategy is simple, "all you got to do is call on them." Pat has noticed that for years, all he has had to do is show up on Tuesday and they will find some order to give him. Sometimes the orders are really good orders. This time is a little different. When Pat stops in to see the PA, he uses his favorite pitch "anything I can help you with?" The PA responds, "Pat, unfortunately, there isn't anything that you can help me with today and there won't be anything that you can help me with again—ever. I appreciate everything you have done for us over the years, but we must cut costs and IMEC came to us with a strategic sourcing proposal that we just couldn't refuse. All of our business will go to them from now on."

Pat's confidence has really been shaken now. So he goes to see another of his favorite contractors. A big lighting job has been on the streets for a couple of weeks and Pat needs to see where things stand. He knows he should have a good number, because he practically gave the stuff away. He and his inside salesman must have put a hundred hours into that quote. Pat talks to the owner, with whom he has a great relationship. Of course, the owner tells him that he was just *barely* edged out by FJBSH on the bid. Pat is thinking "Darn those FJBSH people", don't they know how to make a decent profit? I practically gave the stuff away and they still beat me! As Pat is leaving, the owner asks him one more question—"hey Pat, have you guys ever considered having one of those project management departments like FJBSH has?"

Beaten enough for one day, Pat heads back to the office of his profit center—"We don't really know what it is that we do Electrical Supplies." Upon arriving, Pat goes to his manager, Gomer, with a few suggestions that he has come up with on his drive back to the office. "Hey Gomer, I have a question—why can't we combine the purchasing power of our entire company so we can buy as competitively as TBCP&WH? We just lost a sizable wire order to them and the customer didn't even give us a shot because he knew we couldn't compete.

Gomer makes a note on his list of things to talk to his Division Manager about:

- *Combine our purchasing power*

Then Pat adds, "Got killed by another national account deal today. That's right, IMEC just took another one right off the face of the earth." Gomer thinks about that and responds, "But IMEC is a local independent. How did they do that?" Pat quickly responds, "well it wasn't national, but it was...just like it; you know,--all the bells and whistles."

Gomer's DM notes now read:

- *Combine our purchasing power*
- *National account initiative*

Then Gomer asks Pat about the BIG order. Pat tells him that, even with the nano-margins that they quoted, they were still beat by FJBSH. Then Pat asks one final question, "Have we ever thought about having a project management department?"

Gomer's notes:

- *Combine our purchasing power*
- *National account initiative*
- *Competition taking orders at less than 1%*
- *Project management department*
- *Follow up to question about cutting head count. Can't do it—people are too busy as it is. Can hardly keep up.*

Pat, and now Gomer are having a really, really bad day.

WHY IT IS SO IMPORTANT THAT PC MANAGERS CALL ON CUSTOMERS

Anyone who has been a PC manager for any amount of time has heard some speech about the importance of getting out and seeing customers. I have given hundreds of those speeches myself. So why am I writing this paper? Because I think many managers don't understand all of the reasons why it is so important, or what they are trying to accomplish in establishing these relationships.

An obvious reason that managers should call on customers is to get business. Many people can provide the field sales function. But look at what happens to the cost structure of the profit center if the manager provides those services and doesn't have to pay someone else to do it. In a small profit center where there is only need for one outside salesman, whether the manager does it or has to pay someone else to do it can mean the difference between success and failure. Another reason that the manager should call on customers for the purpose of selling is that he *should* be the best salesman he has.

The rest of the story...

Learn how to run your PC.

Other reasons that a manager should call on customers are less obvious, but probably more important. The first is to learn how to run the business. There are companies out there that spend millions of dollars on consultants to discover what their customers want. The effectiveness of those millions of dollars pales in comparison to the *power* of a local entrepreneur having a businessman-to-businessman discussion about how his profit center should run and then going back to that very same profit center and running it that way.

You have an extraordinary competitive advantage as a Manager of a CED profit center and to succeed it is imperative that you use that advantage. As a CED PC Manager, you have the ability to make the decisions, (financial and otherwise) on how to run your profit center based specifically on the needs of *your* chosen customers. This is huge. You are in the middle of it, so you probably don't see it, sort of how a fish doesn't know that it is in the water. But if you were to go spend time with most of our competitors, (certain local independents excluded), you would see with the same startling reality what a fish does...just after tasting air for the first time, that your competition makes these decisions in distinctly different places. With most of your competition, branch-operations are responsible for sales/marketing and the customer interface. Then, in some remote area across the country or even across the Atlantic, someone else decides how to run the company and how to allocate resources.

This gives you an incredible opportunity. There are two things that you must do to take advantage of it. First, use your time with your customers to find out how you should be running your profit center and run your profit center that way.

Second, remember that CED has given you this great competitive advantage of being the same person in your financial management role as the person that has the customer relationship. Where your competition may separate those two roles by states or oceans, you are one person, but could you not unwittingly emulate their model to your detriment? If you get out there in front of your customer and find out what he or she needs in great detail, then go into your office and get out your P&L to decide how to run your business, are you any different? If you are going to do it that way, just let your Division Manager do it. Let me be more specific. Let's say that you have chosen the perfect customer and found out what their needs are. The customer needs you to be ready to deliver 30-200 amp disconnects with a few hours notice. To do that you need the disconnects, a truck, and a driver. You go back and read your P&L and it tells you that your turns are 5.1, (because you are stocking too many things that you don't need), so you decide that maybe you could keep 10 disconnects on the shelf to get the customer by while you get the rest in. I can tell you how this story ends. The customer tries you twice, and realizing that you can't handle his business, leaves. You are left with way too many 200 amp disconnects, further bloating your inventory and landing on write-down.

It is important to note that, since a manager isn't calling on customers just to sell, he shouldn't limit the customers he calls on to only those who are unassigned. For that matter, he should make sure that he has the primary relationship with those customers. I will never forget the time when I was in the eleventh hour of closing a multi-million dollar single source contract with a large refinery. My salesman had been calling on the account for many years and had great relationships with everyone at the account. I am sure that they all loved him. The day before the final decision was made, the head of procurement called me and said, "What if I told you that for you to get this business, you are going to have to give us a different salesman"? Of course, you know how I responded. The point is what if I had not had the relationship that I did with the customer? What if I had left it all up to the outside salesman? I would have been doomed. Examples such as this make me a big believer in the PC manager having the primary business relationship with the customer, whether the account is assigned to a salesman or not.

I have been using the phrase "call on customers" throughout this article, but the contact and relationship can happen in other ways, such as at the counter or over the phone. Just remember that it is something more than just a sell/buy relationship.

The businessman-to-businessman relationship

Another very important reason that a PC Manager should call on customers is to develop that businessman-to-businessman *relationship* with the customer. Let's look at an example to illustrate the point. You have two independent manufacturers' reps that you do business with. Like all reps, they have their good days and their bad days. They have their good people and their bad people. Sometimes you get answers, sometimes you don't. Now, let's say that with one of the rep agencies, you have a personal relationship with the principle of the firm. You know him well and feel comfortable that he is on your side. He has made it clear that if you ever have a problem, let him know and he will take care of it. Now it is a whole new ball game—a different kind of relationship. With that agency, you know that any apparent shortcomings aren't on purpose and that if you get tired of something, you can just call the owner and he will take care of it. You can even feel a sense of ownership in the service package that you are receiving. With that other agency and no relationship, you are on your own and when you have had enough, you have no choice but to find another supplier.

It is the same with your PC and your relationship to your customers. It is even easier for you to create a competitive advantage than it is for the independent rep. With the reps, any one of them can just choose whether or not to have a relationship with you. On the other hand, with most of your competition, the guy that is making the decisions that can impact a customer is so far removed (like in France), that he will never have that relationship.

To put one final point on it, Haygemeyer just decided that the best thing for all their customers in North America is Phillips lamps and P&S wiring devices. You, on the other hand could decide to supply all custom-made nickel plated EMT fittings if you wanted to because that is what your customer told you they needed, (that would be a pretty hefty premium, by the way).

There is an important lesson to remember here. As the profit center manager of a CED profit center, *you are in charge*. I know that most of you are thinking, "I know that" and I don't doubt that you do. The reason I am making the point is, though you believe that you are in charge, you might not realize how easy it is to undermine your own authority. Quite often, the apparent easy way to deal with something is to put the responsibility on someone else. Statements like "against corporate policy", or "my division manager didn't approve that raise", "we are not allowed to have a lot of inventory" completely eliminates your strongest competitive advantage—that you are in charge of your profit center. And once you eliminate your own authority, it is almost impossible to get it back. The rule that I think a profit center manager should live by is that to employees, vendors, and customers, ***you*** should be perceived as the highest level of authority in the company.

The all important employee buy-in

As you get further into these articles, you are going to start running into two important recurring themes. One is that often we, as managers, have our opinions as to how things should work, but they are only opinions. That doesn't make them the facts. The second related theme is that you won't make any progress with any of this stuff by understanding it in only your mind. You must get the rest of the crew to have the same vision as you and to "buy-in" to what you are telling them needs to be done. Think of those two challenges and consider this. How much easier would it be to gain your employees' buy-in if, rather than telling them your opinions, you are telling them *exactly* what the customer told you that they want. I could see someone arguing with a boss that says "those trucks need to be out of here by 8:00". But would they argue with "Bob says that a key element of our maintaining his business, is to consistently get his material to his shop by 8:00".

It is important to call on customers and hey, feel free to sell something while you are there. But remember that there are other, even more important reasons why you are making those sales calls.

Hold on—it's not that simple!

I could see how a reader could read this article on why managers should call on customers and think, "that's a neat trick. I could see how that could help us. I'll have to do some of that one day, but today, I am working on getting rid of these write-downs." The thing is, ***you have no choice but to do it.*** Here's why. With most of your chain competitors and even many of the independents, when they get their little "branch in a box" kit to run, it includes something called a value proposition--a reason to buy from them. Sure, it is crudely written in far away places like St. Louis, Pittsburgh, or France, but it is something. When you get the CED, "profit center in a box" kit, it doesn't include a value proposition. There is nothing in the box that is intended to make you good to your customers. *You* must create the value proposition. If you do, and you do it based on feedback from your chosen customers, you will have a great advantage over your competitors. But if you don't, you are at a disadvantage.

Last but not least, find the good talent in the market

The last valuable reason for a PC Manager to call on customers and that is to determine where the good talent is in the market. Your customers, who deal with your competition, know better than anyone else who the great inside sales people are in your market. Your customers know who is unhappy with their boss and who is ready for the next larger opportunity. Your customers also know you and could provide a "reference" to potential employee candidates about the great qualities of the local CED and its manager.

SALES STRATEGY MISTAKES

My experience has led me to develop a theory that most mistakes that are made with sales strategies are caused by people having a certain paradigm about how sales occur and, as a result, relying on a particular strategy that is not applicable to what they are trying to accomplish. To make the point, let's first look at the reasons a sale gets made.

- **Because you are there.** Sometimes a sale is successfully made because a salesman was in front of a buyer asking for an order when the buyer had an order to place and no one else was there. Another way this strategy can manifest itself is through the location of a distributor. Just another way of being there. If a distributor is located in a particular city, or part of a city, where people might need to buy things and no one else is located there, that distributor will tend to get business based on that location. This can also apply at an even smaller level. You might not be the only one **"there"**, but you are the only one there with a particular product, meaning you were in front of the buyer as the distributor of a particular line, or you are in a particular location with a particular line and no one else is. There is nothing wrong with getting business because you are there (until someone else gets there). The confusion comes in when you start thinking that, because you are there, that customers appreciate the value that you bring to the market and will give you business even when you are not there, or when someone else is also **"there"**.

- **Because you asked.** Sometimes, all things being equal, the guy who asks for the order gets it.
- **Because of relationships.** Relationships are necessary to facilitate the introduction of the customer to the profit center. If most of the rest of the selling equation is the same, the one with the best relationship will have a better chance of writing the business. Sometimes, relationships can even overcome deficiencies between one company and another. But one must be careful not to get in a situation where all the sales force does is use their relationships to gain *forgiveness* for what we did for the customer this time. Remember, an outside salesman is paid to be a magician that can pull the rabbit out of the hat; but only if there is a rabbit in the hat in the first place. And remember, business based largely on a salesman's relationship is very vulnerable for the profit center.
- **Because of price.** Again, all things being equal, the lower price will win the business.

- **Because a distributor had the superior value/service offering (SV/SO).** In other words, a distributor was really and truly the better choice for the customer. In those previous bullets, the phrase "all things being equal" refers to the value/service offering. It is what makes things equal or not. The SV/SO is discussed in greater detail in the article on Customer Service.
- **Because the distributor that has the business hasn't lost it yet.** Every distributor has many customers that would change to a better supplier if they thought there was one out there. This makes two good arguments. On the one hand, you want to make sure that you are doing the right job for your customers to ensure that you keep them. Just because you haven't lost a particular customer yet, doesn't mean that you won't. On the other hand, this makes a good case for getting into a strong number two position at a customer that is within your focus and waiting for the number one supplier to drop the ball (they almost always do). Of course, getting into that number two slot will only be productive if you have an equal or **superior value/service offering**.

So if you want to successfully sell (whatever that means to your organization), and you believe that the previously listed bullets are all of the reasons that things get sold, then you want to make sure that your organization has exactly the right balance of all of the above ingredients. That balance will change with each selling situation. Your organization will need to be in the right number of the right places, asking for orders more than the next guy, with really good customer relationships, at the right price (or in certain cases a low price), with a **value/service offering** that is better than the competition.

Now for the mistakes

How do we fail? It is usually because people have succeeded at some point in the past with one of the above strategies and now erroneously believes that is the only path to success. A classic example is the **there** strategy. Any of us who have been in the field sales arena has gone to a customer, possibly a new one and said something like "is there anything I can help you with" and got an order. Though that is a purely random strategy, I would never propose to an organization that they make themselves completely void of such an approach. However, it probably won't work with the other 95% of the customers. Rarely is it the case that the competitive landscape is so balanced that just showing up wins. I would also argue that the level of success of that approach is falling over time. Years ago, customers knew less about their buying options and, I believe, just plain needed less from a supplier than they do today.

While we are on the subject of customers needing less (or having lower expectations) than they do today, let's look at the **relationship** strategy. I would certainly agree that customer relationships will go a long way to ensure that a supplier gets at least an even shot at writing business, and in some cases an unfair advantage—which can be good. But let's look at an example of how relying solely on that approach can be deadly. Years ago, there were all these motor freight carriers. They were all pretty bad at what they did. You never knew when your product would actually arrive or what condition it would be in. Their billing was less reliable than playing roulette. How did customers choose one carrier over another? I will tell you how I did it. The customer that had the most congenial representative calls on me the most often. So they used the **there** strategy and the **relationship** strategy. But they forgot the **superior value/service offering** strategy. I also gave some business to the postal service that used only the **there** strategy. Then FedEx showed up. The FedEx strategy, as I am sure you know, was purely the **superior value/service offering.** Now relationships are out the window as is **price**. I use FedEx because it "absolutely has to be there." Sorry motor freight guys.

I don't mean to understate the value of relationships in the selling process. In fact, relationships are necessary to get the customer to consider all of the other things in the equation. The point I am trying to make here is that relationships can't replace everything else. We can all think of times when getting the order was all about relationships and nothing else. You have to remember that in those times, the customer expectations were such that many of the competitors could provide the level of service required.

Another way that people get fooled into thinking that relationships are everything is when the salesman--who we associate with relationships--is actually *providing* the **superior value/service offering**. In other words, the salesman is single handedly making the supply house better than it really is. He is doing expediting and order follow up. He might even act as his own inside salesman. If you let yourself get into the situation where you are the "not very good" supplier that relies solely on the sales force's relationships skills, you are probably in for trouble.

There is a real life lesson to remember here. It has to do with the subject of hiring a salesman from the competition. You know how you always go through the part about "he can bring 4 million dollars with him?" Assuming that you buy in to some of the previous points, let's think about the "bring the business scenario" for a minute. If that salesman provides both the value and the relationship, then he might be able to bring that business. If he only provides the relationship, then it is a different story. In the second case, whether he can bring any business depends on how your **superior value/service offering** stacks up to that of the competition.

Another classic mistake that is made is the **ask for the order** strategy. We have all won orders because, while everything was equal or close to it, we asked for the order. If you are like me, you have also lost a few because you didn't and someone else did. Where people go wrong is they forget that this strategy only works when the field is relatively level.

My most amusing, and annoying manifestation of this mistake is the rep who just botched up everything he could about the order you placed with him last week and asks you for another order, even though the problems with the last order still haven't been resolved. He is using the high **there,** high **ask,** zero **superior value** plan. For that plan to work, he had better have some pretty bad competitors. So like relationships, make sure you have asking for the order within your repertoire, but don't think that is the solution when other things are missing.

Another amusing example of the **ask** fallacy is with Allen-Bradley distributors. When they sell a PLC or a Drive, they offer the customer a **value/service offering** that is second to none. They know the products; can educate the customer on what the products are and how to apply them. They have everything in stock and could practically install the product if needed. Yet, watch that same Allen-Bradley distributor put together a strategy to sell any other product, like lighting. What is their entire strategy? "You just got to **ask** for that other stuff!" What they don't realize is that the competition is just as good at lighting as they are at PLC's. How successful is the lighting distributor at going to an industrial and asking for a shot at the PCL business.

The same goes for losing orders. Remember Gomer – he thought it was price.

Putting the theory into practice

So how can motivated readers put this theory to good use? There are two things to consider. First, if you look at any salesman or selling situation, there is usually a strong bias toward one of the strategies while virtually ignoring others. You will see the guy who only leads with **price**. There is the **relationship** guy who never follows through. There is the guy who always **asks** for the order, whether he is in a position to write it or not. There is the milk run guy who just **shows up** a lot. In defense of these people, most of their bias and blind spots are due to either personal weakness (poor attention to detail, or inability to build relationships), or more often, their past successes. They wrote a great order or pulled in a great account just because they were **there.** The enlightenment I would want to give anyone with those biases and blind spots is to remember that in those situations where that one strategy worked, they were probably on a fairly even playing field when judged against the competition. But today, the playing field may often not be level.

The right thing for a manager to do is to manage the sales force and remember these points in the process. In your daily conversations with the salesmen, find out which area he is biased toward and move him back to center. *(You **are** having regular conversations with your salespeople, aren't you?)*

The second advice I would give is to always focus on, at least, leveling the playing field, but preferably tilting it in a direction that puts you at an advantage. This gets to the universal value of the **superior value/service offering** strategy. In other words, remember the FedEx trick. If you build your organization so that you are, more often than not, the absolute best solution for your customer, everything else becomes easy. (Of course, being the absolute best solution to a particular customer base requires that you have a well thought out and focused customer base, but that requires another article). Maybe you just leave it at that. Do the FedEx thing and have a higher price and no relationships. But if you need to do more, you can add relationships, the right price, and even asking for the order. In contrast, if you start with one of the other strategies as your foundation, you will be hard pressed to expand your success beyond that.

If you take your target customer list and evaluate your success at each account, then compare your situation with the ways listed above as to how you can write an order, you will probably see the deficiency that is causing you to be less successful than you might be otherwise. Typically, a given supply house will have a certain deficiency that is common with many customers. My experience has been that, most often, the deficiency lies in the **superior service/value offering** area. Yours may be different. However, if you can identify the blind spot in your organization or in certain people within your organization, you will make all of the other areas more successful and more efficient.

CUSTOMER SERVICE

The purpose of this essay is to cover the subject of customer service, what it is, why it is important, how to give it, and to do so in as few pages as possible.

What it is.

As electrical distributors, we provide parts. Our competitors do the same thing. Customer service is everything else that we do that makes those transactions better for the customer and as a result, makes us better than the competition. Customer service begins somewhere before we take an order and ends somewhere after the bill is paid.

Why you need great customer service, (or a superior value/service offering (SV/SO)

Superior customer service is a primary driver of profitability in these ways:

1. It is more efficient to serve customers correctly than it is to serve them incorrectly, (you know, do it right the first time).

2. Superior customer service facilitates deeper customer penetration. It also improves customer retention which is good because customers get more profitable over time.
3. As you read in "Sales Strategy Mistakes", there are a number of ways to get a customer's business. You could be "there more often", or lower your "price" or "ask" for the order, etc. All of these are more expensive than having a superior value/service offering, or customer service. Another way to look at this is that it is more expensive to pay the field sales function to constantly repair the damage done by handling a transaction poorly, than it is to just pay them to get business.

The point is that doing what is necessary to provide superior customer service does not increase costs--it increases *profitability*.

I suspect that some readers at this point in this article might be saying to themselves, "great...I agree 100% with what he is saying. That is good for us too, because we have the best service in town!" If you are one of those readers, you are not exactly out of the woods, *yet*. The problem is, every distributor on the planet says the same thing. What most distributors really mean when they say they have the best service is that they have a service *culture*, which we will talk about in a minute. The fact of the matter is, the service that most distributors have is just "randomly generated".

Random Customer Service

Most distributors (and people) tend to focus on a certain aspect of customer service and have blind spots in other areas of customer service. Those areas of focus may be carefully calculated or rather random (mostly random). An example of the focus/blind spot dynamic is a distributor may truly excel in on- time deliveries out of stock, but do poorly in back-order management.

When I say that some distributors tend to "focus" on a certain aspect, and that they sometimes do so at "random", that can happen in a number of ways. In some cases, a distributor does actually focus on certain areas of customer service, but the reason for doing so is really nothing more than certain people having certain biases, rather than because their customers want them to do so. This is the manager that is obsessed with the trucks leaving before 8:00AM, or the phone being answered on the third ring, yet that same manager is oblivious to order pulling accuracy or response time on quotes. Another "random focus" is not even focus at all. It is just that that is the way things are. In other words, the experienced counter man, who once was an electrician, does a great job of helping each customer make sure that they order what they need. Or, the super attention to detail inside person, who looks through all open orders for her customers every day and follows up to make sure that everything is still on time.

It is great that these things happen, but it is a strategy more akin to *luck* than anything else. The sum total of all of this random customer service is a random business with random customer retention. I know this sounds like an attempt at humor, but when you really look at it, how often do we do what we want and customers separately need what they need, and the two just happen to match up? When it does, we keep a customer and when it doesn't we don't. Random focus, random customer service, and random customer retention are all fine, and as a matter of fact, that is the way many relationships are. *As long as you don't mind random profitability.*

Many managers in our industry go through their entire career not realizing that even though they are attempting to provide great customer service, their entire service strategy is random. How do they do that? They are continually looking for that set of employees that left to their own devices, will collectively provide great service to the customer. That is OK, but it sure seems hard. Seems to me like McDonalds searching the earth, looking for someone who can cook a hamburger well.

Rising above the pack with your SV/SO

To rise above the rest of the crowd with you customer service or SV/SO, you must first understand *where* it is happening. Customer service for an electrical distributor "happens" at these points:

- Order entry—via phone, fax, e-mail, etc.
- Providing price and availability
- Sourcing special order material
- Counter Sales
- Inside technical support
- Product availability, inventory management
- Project management
- Order tracking and expediting
- Backorder management
- Order pulling
- Delivery
- Returns
- Problem resolution and prompt issuance of credit memos
- Collection

A good elementary exercise to try in your profit center would be to take each of the above components and judge your capabilities against what you would expect that your customers want. Do you have a plan for backorder management, or answering the phone?

Of course, how good you are at each of these is dependent upon the unique needs of the customers in your focus group (which means you need to know what your focus is). For example, a residential supply house must be excellent at inventory management and fill rates, but doesn't need to be so good at backorder management. Regardless of what they are, you have a set of customer service parameters that are important to one degree or another to your chosen customer base. Now you have to ensure that you have the three pillars of customer service: **culture**, **systems**, and **effort** to support those parameters.

The three pillars of customer service.

When I describe the three components of customer service, you should quickly see that most people (maybe you) focus on certain areas and have blind spots in others. I like to think of the three areas of customer service as a pyramid, as one builds on the other.

A Customer Service Culture

The bottom layer of the pyramid would be a *defined customer service culture*. Management must drive excellence in all of the areas in the bullets above, or those that management chooses. These critical points are talked about in meetings and describe how we differentiate ourselves from the competition. All those trite phrases that you can think of right now that include the word service are what I am talking about in this bottom level. My favorite is the line that every single electrical distributor on the planet uses "Our customers buy from us because of our service". I can call this very necessary level of the pyramid the "base" level because it is absolutely necessary, however, the only problem is that everybody has it. It is about as much of a differentiator as extension of credit.

The one exception I would make to the above statement is that, though everyone talks about service, not everyone talks about exactly what it is. And if you don't define it, you don't have it. So we need to be specific in talking about superior service in terms such as enhanced inventory management, or answering the phone.

Systems (or processes)

The next layer of the customer service pyramid is *systems* to ensure customer service delivery. Everything that happens in a profit center happens because of systems. As a result, everything that happens--happens exactly according to plan. I am betting that there is a high percentage of you that are thinking right now, "This guy is crazy. I just had three things this morning that didn't go *according to plan!"* Let's take a closer look at those plans (processes).

You hire a relatively unintelligent guy to work in the warehouse and train him for the usual ten minutes. Then you give him order-pulling responsibility and don't really have a process for double-checking orders. An order gets pulled and shipped wrong. The plan worked perfectly.

Another, more common example is with expediting. A customer orders a special order product. The salesman doesn't ask the customer when he needs the material. He faxes an order to the supplier and never even checks to see if the supplier received the order. As far as he knows, the order fell behind the back of the fax machine. He also doesn't know if the supplier had the material in stock or if they did, when they expect to ship it. An irate customer calls when the material doesn't come in as expected. Again, the plan worked perfectly.

Let's say you have a "cash cow" customer that fires you and goes to another supplier. He does so because he can never get his inside sales person on the phone. He can't get his inside person on the phone because she is always on the phone with a "BSL", or she is busy ordering material that should have been in stock. The cash cow doesn't know who to call to complain. Again, this is perfectly according to plan.

Different levels of systems

For anything, there can be different levels (or degrees) of systems. To illustrate, look at something simple like getting the lights in the warehouse turned on everyday. The lowest level would be no system at all. It goes like this: Manager tells no one anything and no one knows who is supposed to turn the lights on. Some employees are conscientious enough to turn the lights on, but they are not always there. That means that sometimes the lights aren't on in the morning. When the manager goes in the dark warehouse, he says something like, "you would think we could get some people that had enough sense to turn the (bleeping) lights on in the morning."

The next level up is to make turning the lights on an expectation and to tell someone in the profit center that that is their responsibility. You might even have a back-up plan in case that person is out for some reason.

Ratcheting up one more level would be to take one of those Tork 24-hour timers that are on display at your counter and hook it so that the lights come on everyday at the same time.

Let's take a simple electrical distribution example like providing a price. Just assume that customers want their price requests to be quick, reliable, and accurate. What systems do we have to deliver that? Here is a quick list.

- A solid price matrix.
- Quickly accessible info on prices for non-stock items.
- Consistent pricing strategies among the sales staff.

Of course, if you want to beat that baseline level of performance then you have to evolve into other things like having established pricing with the customer loaded into their system, so that the customer doesn't even need to ask the price. Ask yourself, do you know your customers' expectation relative to providing price and availability? Do you meet *those* expectations?

Providing a price is one of the simplest examples. Other customer service issues can be more complex such as the subject of systems necessary to provide strong performance on back-order management or project management. Certainly a little trickier than pricing, but still it is relatively simple to set up the proper systems to ensure high quality customer service in that area.

The customer service improvement process

To ensure that you are optimizing your systems to provide a superior value/service offering, take the bullets listed above on *where* customer service happens and do this:

1. Pick one of the items, like answering the phone.
2. Understand the definition of great customer service in the eyes of your customers. Of course, you will probably need to ask them to gain that understanding. (And of course, it you have all different kinds of customers, you will get all kinds of answers.)
3. Once you know the definition of "great", ask yourself and your team this—*"what compelling reason do we have to believe that our performance in this area is more appealing to our customers than our competition?"*
4. Adjust your systems as necessary to achieve the level of success that you desire to achieve in (3) above. Write these down as necessary.
5. Make sure that everyone in the profit center knows the new plan.

6. As necessary, measure and monitor the new process to ensure that you are achieving the desired level of success.
7. Check back with those customers you asked and see if you are doing better.

This will surely give you a leg up on the competition. But that doesn't mean that nothing will ever go wrong again. You are probably on a multi-year journey and even when you fix things, the unexpected can happen. That is why you need additional plans for *"extra effort."*

Extra Effort

The systems to deliver customer service and extra effort go hand in hand. You shouldn't have just one. Extra effort is what an employee does when something goes wrong. Things didn't go as planned (or weren't planned), and now we have a big problem. Extra effort makes systems work better. Better systems reduce the need for extra effort. You always want to think about whether your systems are really systems at all, or just one "extra effort" after another.

When something does go wrong, an employee can deal with the customer in a couple of ways. One is the "sorry pal" approach, which, of course, doesn't work. And I know that no one really says "sorry pal", but they do say something like, "that is the way things are." In other words, how could we deliver that today, when our truck doesn't go there until tomorrow? Another approach is "I have to check with management", and lets not forget "blame the vendor". The consistent message is "too bad there is a problem; you are just going to have to deal with it".

The preferred situation is for the employee, whoever they are, to just solve the problem. I don't mean solve the problem if it costs less than $50 to solve the problem. I mean *solve* the problem.

So the three switchboards are going to ship a week late, which will put the contractor in a big bind. The salesman can blame the vendor, say sorry pal, go check with management; or, say, "Sorry we didn't get it done for you on this one. I will be glad to FedEx those panels in so they will be here tomorrow and I will follow up to see what went wrong so it doesn't happen again." I know such a reaction seems perfectly fine and that anyone would expect things to happen that way. Unfortunately, I have seen too many times where an inside salesman bought something from a competitor to take care of a customer and then was reprimanded by the Profit Center manager for losing money on the ticket.

Many of you might be thinking, it would cost way too much money to do that with all my customers all the time. I agree. You are right. So only do it with your profitable customers.

My advice to you as a take away from this section on "extra effort" is to ensure that your employees know who you intend to provide great service to and that they also know the amount of latitude they have to solve any problem that may arise.

- Customer service increases profitability, not costs.
- Know the things that impact customer service and what your customer's standards are for those items.
- Make sure that you are addressing all (3) elements of customer service, **culture, systems, extra effort.**
- Always ask, "what compelling reason do we have to believe that our performance in this area is more appealing to our customers than our competition?"

MARKET FOCUS

So you have bought into the concept of Market Focus... Now, what do you do about it?

If you read the section on customer service and thought to yourself, man that is a lot of work. I am supposed to find out what those scores of different customers want? That will take forever! I have a solution for you. Don't try. In this section on market focus, we are going to talk about how you can do a much better job if you only pick one or two customer types (and their needs) to work on.

Market Focus

It seems at first like this subject, Market Focus, is one of those where there is a large gap between buy-in and successful implementation. The purpose of this article is to cover the things that a profit center manager can do to be 90% good in this area without making it so complicated that it never gets done.

Market Focus is deciding what you want to do well and doing that more often than other things. This is all about profitability and companies operate more profitably *within* their focus. It would make sense then that one would want to know what their focus is, so they can devote the maximum time and energy to that focus in order to continually improve. Let's look at a real world example. In this case, we will use UPS.

UPS is in the service business, more specifically in the service business of shipping (certain) packages efficiently around the world in a timely manner and at a fair price. Now that we have said that, UPS knows what it is they should do all day. They should, a) ship packages and, b) get better at shipping packages. All questions that could come up in a day are easily answered. See how elegantly simple that is? If UPS is faced with a decision to ship yet another package, their decision is easy and it will probably be a profitable endeavor for them. Why? Because shipping another package is simply doing what they already do very well--again.

Now let's look at an example where UPS decides to provide a service that is not part of their market focus. How about providing Chiropractic care? Boy are they in a pickle now! Their drivers who were really good at driving and dropping off packages are now no longer qualified. They have to be retrained or replaced. And it is likely that people that provide quality Chiropractic care don't drive big brown trucks well. Those brown trucks that are perfectly suited to delivering packages are poorly suited to providing Chiropractics, and besides, packages would be falling all over the patients. I think you get the point.

Extreme example-*or is it?*

You may say that the UPS illustration was an extreme example, so let's translate it to Electrical Distribution. Let's say your market focus is to provide cheap residential wiring devices to residential contractors that want them. How do you run your business? Let's see. For a device line I would pick cheap and residential. For a building let's go small--receptacles aren't that big. Delivery vehicles would be small and cheap. Quality of the inside sales force? Who cares? Get cheap clerks. And what do you do when you come in to work every morning? That's right; you make sure that you have plenty of cheap residential wiring devices on the shelf.

Now let's make it more complicated. Let's add to the above focus selling devices to just about any customer that buys wiring devices and let's also sell them the boxes that they go in (Let's keep in mind that this is still much less complicated than your typical electrical supply house!). Now answer the same questions. Device line--well, you need the cheap stuff for the resi-guys, but you also need a full industrial line. Of course, the industrial manufacturer doesn't like to share with the resi-type manufacturer and the resi manufacturer always wants a piece of the industrial and twist lock type of business. Both manufacturers consider commercial and hospital grade a core product that they don't want to give up to the other guy. Maybe you can get a full line that does both. Will that take you out of the industrial market because you have a wiring device line that isn't really recognized in that area? Guess you will need to add some outside salespeople to go out and convince those customers that your alternate line is just as good.

What about the delivery vehicles and building? Need much bigger ones to carry all those boxes. The sales force needs to be smarter and better educated to deal with all those twist lock part numbers. And what do you do when you get to work in the morning? Any number of things, like work on your purchasing procedures. And by the way, no one may even notice that you are out of almond 15A receptacles today. The fact is you just can't be as good or as profitable as the distributor that is only selling cheap residential devices to residential contractors.

If these two distributors compete in the cheap resi-device arena, who wins? The more focused distributor. He will make more money and do a better job, while penetrating his customer base deeper.

Decide what your focus is

Now, let's get back to real life. How do you apply this to what you are doing today? First, you have to decide what your focus is. If you look at your profit center, you probably have some core identity that is happening already, even if by accident. The customers that like you the best and that you like the best are probably of a similar type, or at least a majority of them are. You have employees, lines, systems and processes, and various other resources that support those favorite customers. Everything about that particular set of customers seems to be a good fit for you and you are a good fit for them. Based on that, here is all you have to do.

- Admit that this is your focus and let everyone know.
- When faced with a decision that supports that focus and makes you better at it, do it.
- When faced with a decision that doesn't support that focus, don't do it.

Using these three simple rules, let's take a test. In this case, you are the cheap resi-device distributor in the market and you have decided that is your focus. The following are some typical management decisions that you might face. How would you answer them?

The Hubble Wiring Device salesman wants to set up a time to come and see you.

One of your employees came to you and said that with your location, you could get a lot of good walk-in business if you set up some merchandising.

You heard that the heavy hitter outside salesman with the competition is looking to make a move and wants to talk to you.

Your Leviton salesman (that's your line) said that if you would place an order for an extra $10,000 he would give you an exclusive 20% discount.

You heard about the new black devices and wonder if you should invest in them.

Watch how long it takes to make those decisions. Nope, nope, nope, yes, yes. Easy, isn't it?

Why do it the easy way when you can do it the hard way?

What happens, instead of this simple life, is that you usually haven't decided what it is you want to be. Thus, all decisions are more complicated because they include with every one of them "Do I want to get more into that market or do I want to get more out of it" and "If I do that it will help with "these" customers, but will hurt with "those" customers. You keep wasting time talking to the Hubbell guy or setting up counter displays for no reason. Decisions are more complicated because there are always pro's and con's. *Actually, you find yourself just making changes and **hoping** it will make things better.*

I know what you are saying. You are saying, "When I look at my current situation, it just isn't that simple. I have a $50k break-even and I am running an average of $48k/month GP. How can I get rid of the 30% of my customers that aren't part of my focus?" Well, don't. Just stop building your business around customers that aren't within your focus. Don't try to be competitive, if they buy, make them *pay*. Don't assign an outside salesman to them. Don't make inventory or line decisions because of them. Don't make any decision about how to run your business because of them. Always run your business based upon your market focus. *Don't make your chosen customers wait while you serve them.*

Here is what will happen when you focus.

1. Your costs will go down—because you will stop spending money to support customers outside your focus.
2. You will lose business and customers outside of your focus because you are not investing in that market any longer.
3. Losing this non-focus business and customers will free up additional capacity (future article), causing you to further penetrate the customers within your focus, resulting in profits rising.
4. You will spend more time in your new simple life, getting better at servicing your customers within your focus, further enhancing your "penetration" and profits.

There is focus and there is taking orders

A not so subtle point that must be made is the difference between focus and taking orders. Say you are that resi-device distributor and you get a call from a customer that is building a tennis court in his back yard and wants 10 sportslighter fixtures. Assuming you have someone who knows what that is, that you have a place to buy them, and most importantly, that you won't have to take resources away from serving your target customer base, then maybe you should take the order and make 40% on it. Normally however, this is not the case. Most typically, you have to take resources away from serving your target customer base to handle that order that is outside of your focus. Next thing you know, your favorite resi-device customers are holding on the phone to wait for an inside salesman that is fumbling around looking for tennis court lights. Also, what usually happens is that you start building our business around that non-focused area. You assign specific resources to serve that non-focus area and off you go down the path of becoming a poorly focused distributor.

One could conclude from the previous paragraph that the better a profit center team is at knowing what its target market is and who its target customers are, the better their chances of taking some out of focus orders without hurting anything.

Nothing to focus on?

In many cases, market focus is really just as simple as determining what that profitable core business is within your business and choosing to support that core while letting the rest go. But sometimes it isn't that simple because either there really isn't a profitable core (anymore), or there is an opportunity to be more aggressive by becoming focused quickly.

An example of this would be where you are new in a market, or your profit center has become so confused over the years that you *might as well* be new in a market because there is no real competitive focus left. In this case, you have to make a conscious decision to choose a market and build a business around that market. Though this is a little more work because it involves a little more than saying no, it is actually more fun and usually more effective. Let's look at an example that often occurs.

How to come from last place and beat "The Big Guys"

You are in a large market and over the years, you (or your profit center) have screwed up everything, leaving you comfortably in last place in any race that there is. Your competition--let's call them "The Big Guys" haven't screwed up nearly as much and, as a result are in first place in many categories. The Big Guys own the large contractor market, dominate residential contractors, and because of their size, have endeavored to get into the commercial/government piece and even have a couple of salesmen calling on industrials. You, on the other hand, are so bad that your market focus has been relegated to selling to customers that don't pay their bills. What can you do now? For every resource you have, The Big Guys have twenty. Their value proposition to the customer is "we don't screw up near as much as the other guys." Your value proposition, on the other hand, is something like "come on, give us another shot...what are the chances that we could screw up ten in a row."

The "flanking" maneuver

After giving it careful thought, you realize that The Big Guys can't possibly spend adequate time managing toward excellence in every market they serve. You also determine that, since your resources are so incredibly limited compared to theirs, you will never match them in every area. Out of desperation, you choose to just try to get one thing right. So you decide to become the best supplier to the small-design/build-commercial contractor-who is within 10 miles-and usually does things like tenant build-outs.

Now look how easy your decisions are, and how effectively you can compete. First of all, your statement to your customer base becomes something like this--"We only devote resources to serving small-design/build etc. contractors. That is our passion. We aren't going to make our living like those distributors serving the resi-contractors, yet come trying to poach some of your business just because you are spending money today. We are spending 60 hours a week trying to be better at serving your market segment. What do we need to do better?"

Now, let's look at your next set of choices:

- You currently have Siemens and C/H because C/H is good at shipping panels fast, and Siemens is preferred for Resi. You cut off Siemens. You also make any number of other line changes because you are now serving one master.

- That salesman that has contacts with 3-4 large contractors--you fire him.
- That inside salesman that spends his day quoting $50,000 bills of material for pipe and wire. Fire him too.
- Your training plan becomes clear. Everybody needs to know how to use the C/H quote program and the basics of photometrics and lighting design.
- Things like bolt on breakers and parabolic lay-ins that you have never stocked because they seemed a little too esoteric for your little money losing operation--put them in stock. In fact, stock anything that would be needed to supply a small design/build job like a warehouse or a tenant build-out.

I could go on and on, but, hopefully, you get the point. Additionally, as a manager, your day would be comprised of making sure that every opportunity to serve one of these focus customers is handled perfectly and if it isn't, determining what needs to be fixed in your operation to do better next time. You will quickly take significant share from "The Big Guys" in your niche. They won't be able to combat you because every decision that they make will involve them taking resources away from another profitable part of their business. And the really neat part is *it will be fun.* You will have a purpose. Your employees will have a purpose. Everyone will be more driven to a common cause.

So what if your market isn't big enough to just sell resi-wiring devices?

How focused you need to be depends on the size of your market, the number of competitors you have, and how *good* you are relative to that market. With that in mind, a pure residential, or even "small-residential-custom home-but not lighting-within a ten mile radius" type focus would be well suited in Chicago, but not in Millinocket, Maine. The "how good you are" part is a subject of focus vs. infrastructure. In other words if you are big enough and good enough (high SV/SO), then you don't need to be as focused. An example of this is a PC that, because of their brilliant focus over the years, has developed quite an aptitude for stocking and shipping a wide array of products. Though they might have gotten there by focusing on the commercial contractor segment, they might decide that maybe a couple of MRO industrial customers would like the fact that, though it isn't their focus, they are the best in town at shipping 30, 2" malleable LB's out of stock. So they take some orders. But remember that they came to have the infrastructure because of their focus. Not the other way around.

Though you can expand your focus a bit as you get bigger, better, and more dominant, always remember the dangerous game you can be playing. Sears became bigger and better and expanded their focus to include more things and more target customers. Then they did it again, and again. Then, one day, BOOM! Say good night Sears—hello Wal-Mart.

A common and often suicidal mistake is to see the really big distributor that is in multiple market segments and mistakenly think that in order to compete; you need to be in all those same markets. *That is wrong.* The only way that you can take market share from a competitor with more infrastructure is to target less of the market than that competitor. **In fact, there is a direct correlation between focus and market penetration-- the greater the focus, the greater the penetration.**

Also, focus is inversely proportional to overall share and sheer size. In other words, the more focused one is, the smaller his total potential market is. Potential is a big word here, because in many markets, there is more than enough potential even within a highly focused niche. Smaller potential and small is not the same thing here. Since focus causes greater penetration, penetrating a smaller market will usually result in more overall business. Look at it this way. Say you and I are each going to attack a sheetrock wall and try to put a hole in it--the bigger the hole, the better. I will use an ice pick and you will use an eight- foot long 2x4 piece of wood, laid sideways against the wall. I will make a hole immediately, though it will be a small one. Then I will make another and another. You can press your 2X4 against that wall all day and all you will do is work. You are attacking too much of the wall at a time to make any progress.

Focus also directly correlates to profitability. High focus equals high profitability. As I typically do, let me use an extreme example to illustrate the point. Let's say that you are in a major market (like Beijing) and your focus is to sell "D" cell batteries to anyone who walks in, buys them and pays cash. On the one hand, that would be a superior profitability model; on the other, it might not allow you to tap quite as much of the market as you would hope. To increase your overall share, you might have to carry some "AA"s and some "C"s. You might have to take credit cards. Every step of the way, you will increase your potential market and lower profitability. Taking this relationship to heart, the extremely high profitability profit center might look for new, tangent areas of focus, while the low profitability profit center would look for ways to increase focus, even if it means being a little smaller for a while.

Focus vs. Critical Mass (as in being big)

A reader, particularly one that is in a market where there are some sizeable competitors might read some of this focus/customer selection stuff and think that the message is that you are supposed to be *small.* Well not exactly, but the subject does deserve comment.

As discussed elsewhere, increasing focus will limit the size of the available market, as will holding higher standards on customer selection. So yes, the available market is smaller. In most markets, that isn't a big deal because there is enough available market within any given focus. In other markets, however, being more focused than your chain or super-regional competitor down the street could limit the available market to a point that you could be smaller. Is that a problem? I say no.

Remember way back in "Why PC Managers should call on customers" we first started discussing the CED advantage of having a value/service offering that was brilliantly custom crafted around a very specific customer base. Having your service offering designed so close to the customer reduces waste and allows you to provide an outstanding level of service and make a high profit. I would liken this process to killing a fly with a fly swatter.

Now let us kill that fly from 100 miles away, or 1000 miles away. Now you are using ICBM missiles to kill the same fly. Many of your competitors are designing their value proposition from so far away they have to throw much more weight (critical mass) at it to get the same job done as you.

Where you might attack a problem like this..."so, Mr. Customer, you say you use 10 of those 90 cri, 5000k lamps per week. And you would like them delivered on Friday. O.K., we will do that." Pretty easy to do. Your competition is using the ICBM approach. They must have tons and tons of lamps and a lot of trucks to magically have what that same customer wants. Tons of lamps means they have to have tons of customers, which means that they can't be that picky about who they sell to. So they have no choice but to be big. You can be big if that comes up. You just don't have to.

Looks like a perfect set-up to me.

Summarizing:

- Focus is inversely proportional to overall available market
- Focus is directly proportional to Market Segment Penetration
- The larger your market, the greater the need to focus
- If you are "Big" and "Good", you don't have to be as focused
- If you are "Smaller" and seek to be "Good", you need more focus

Finally, market focus is about consciously choosing what part of the market you want to go after and developing a plan of action to do that. Once you make that commitment, everything else (like customer service) becomes simple (simpler).

CUSTOMER SELECTION

Next to market focus, Customer Selection may have the biggest impact on how profitable a profit center can be. That doesn't mean that doing well in this area will automatically cause a profit center to be highly profitable, just that doing well is required to have the *potential* to be highly profitable. And yes, that does mean that doing poorly with regard to customer selection could make it impossible to be profitable at all. The purpose of this article is to provide a strategy for developing the profitable customer portfolio you need.

I can't tell you that I have any scientific evidence that supports what is in this article. What I can tell you is that when I talk to highly profitable profit center managers, I hear a lot of talk about who they *won't* do business with. And when I talk to marginally profitable profit center managers, I hear things that sound like "every order is a good order", or "and that's business we never had before."

The three levels of customer profitability

If a typical profit center were to rank its customers by bottom line profit, there would be three classes of customers. The top 20% or so would be the "Cash Cows." This group usually makes up all of the profit that the profit center makes plus some more. The bottom

20% or so would be the "Blood sucking losers". This group loses money, eating up the extra profit that the Cash Cows made. The middle group is the "Conditionally or Marginally Profitable" customers. This group is either slightly profitable or unprofitable depending on the situation (such as the price, or whether they pay their bill on time). To save on keystrokes, let's just call them CC's, CP's, and BSL's.

Customer selection involves determining who your CC, CP, and BSL customers are and then deciding what to do about that.

The following are the components of a customer's profitability to your profit center:

- Margin percentage.
- Ability to pay and pay habits.
- How close the customer's needs fit the profit center's capabilities and market focus. In other words, does the customer need you to do what you are already doing, or something else?
- Whether your service model is important to the customer, or not.
- Order size--it is more profitable to deliver $1000 worth of something than to deliver $1 of something.
- Proximity to the Profit Center or typical delivery routes.
- How well the customer runs his business, i.e., are there many expediting requests or returns? This subject can

require more thought than one might think at first. Not only does it have a great deal of impact on your profitability, but in some cases, you may have to judge not only how profitable the customer is today, but how profitable it will be in the future. The classic example is the start up contractor that might be a bit of a pain today, but could really be a moneymaker for you in the future.

- Methods of transacting business, i.e., are orders just faxed in or is everything quoted?
- Time required to serve the customer.
- Service requirements, such as deliveries or special stocking requirements.
- How the customer treats the profit center, i.e., is it a mutually beneficial relationship or is everything win/lose. *Do you like the customer's attitude?*
- Whether or not a salesman is assigned to the account. Obviously, for a given amount of business from a given customer, profitability will be greater if no salesman is assigned than it will if a salesman is assigned.
- The profit center's position at the account. The number one supplier is going to be in a far more profitable position than the others. This particularly true with CP's!
- The competitive landscape of the customer. This has two components that are very important. They are the number of competitors, and how good you are relative to those

competitors. Let's dissect these two points together. First is the number of competitors. OK, so you find this massive cash cow customer that fits perfectly with your focus and no one else has ever heard of this competitor. Euphoria, right? That is what I am talking about with number of competitors. Of course, that rarely happens. There are some exceptions from time to time, like the trench digging company who happens to buy a few truckloads of PVC conduit every month and doesn't care about the price because laying pipe is a sideline for them. Or sometimes there are export companies, (which, of course most of you wouldn't normally deal with). Take out the profitability. In other words, the bigger they are, the more competitors there will be.

So you say, then I will only deal with 1-man contractors. You might be on to something, except remember that a 1-man contractor probably buys one thing at a time, which moves him down the scale on some of the other profitability metrics. Moving up and down the size scale gets you more and less competition along with more and less volume, particularly in the order size department.

Then you have how good you are. If you are the best in town, you can probably take on any competitor (within your focus) and beat them, while still making a profit. If you are not as good, you probably need to stay away from those who might give you a whipping. (If you think that you are as good as anyone, yet find yourself getting beat more often than not, refer to "Sales Strategy Mistakes", or call Gomer from the intro. To put it another way, it isn't price.

Putting the two together, you want to find customers that are:

> As profitable as possible, yet,
> Don't have too many competitors, and,
> You can beat the competitors that there are most of the time.

The bigger the customer is, the more blood that will be spilt to get their business. If you wish to enter such a bloody battle, make sure that most of the blood that is spilt isn't yours.

It gets more complicated

All of these elements are interactive and none alone determines the profitability of the customer. For example, if you look at margin vs. position at the account vs. whether or not a salesman is assigned to that account; several scenarios can evolve. You can potentially improve one area and hurt another. The net effect could raise or lower your overall profitability at that account. Let's say you have a customer that has a salesman assigned, has relatively low margins, and you are the #2 supplier. You might choose to change it to a house account and raise the prices, which will then put you in the #4 competitive position at the account (because now you are only getting their daily pick-up business, but not their low margin gear orders). However, with higher margins and no salesman the account may make more bottom line profit.

To further complicate matters, different customers can be interactive and can change the profitability of each other. An example of this would be with proximity among customer facilities. Let's say that you have a very large customer that does a great deal of volume with you and is 40 miles away. Because of the size of the customer, you stock a lot of material and buy it at a very competitive price and make deliveries every day. In that same vicinity there are 5 smaller customers that you deliver to while you are delivering to the big customer. Because of the competitive nature of the big customer and the Outside Sales time required, it is probably a break-even customer or a slight loser (CP). However, because of the resources that you now have and are able to deploy to such a remote area, you are able to dominate the other 5 smaller customers and make very nice margins, making them CC's. In this example, if you decided to fire the big, unprofitable customer or just give up position, you would lose profitability at the 5 smaller customers. You would lose the resources that allowed you to deliver large volumes of material that you were able to buy very competitively, and efficiently distribute in a remote area.

It is possible to misunderstand and misapply the idea of customer interactivity as it relates to customer profitability. In the example above, the one customer actually changed the profitability at the other customers. An example where that interactivity doesn't exist would be thinking that because one customer pays extremely well, you can *afford* to have other customers that pay poorly. Or that if you make extremely high margins on one customer, you can sell to others at a low margin. That is merely having one customer's profits subsidize another customer's losses. **In fact, I think it is common to have a profit center that has a few wildly profitable CC's, yet posts just good performance because it has a number of BSL's.** Take the BSL's out of the picture that are sucking up all that additional profit and you have a *wildly* profitable profit center. In fact, understanding this concept of cross-subsidization of profits between customers is the single most important concept if you want to be successful at customer selection. The whole idea is to maximize the profit at the profitable customers while not wasting it on unprofitable ones.

There can also be profitability interactivity *within* a customer. In other words, much of their business may be wildly profitable, but some may not be profitable at all. This is OK in many cases. What you have to consider here is, whether having one is worth putting up with the other and what are the consequences of letting the unprofitable part go. An example of a manager not understanding this concept is when upon reviewing the sales ticket of a customer that make the profit center more money than any other customer, the manager questions the one ticket that is not a money maker.

If you are one who reads the various trade magazines and maybe an article from an industry consultant from time to time, you surely have come across a paper that proposes mathematical models to measure customer profitability. The articles will discuss things like "margin contribution", as in how much a customer contributes to your bottom line, or "activity based costing", the process of determining the cost of serving a customer. I am not a strong proponent of such measurement techniques, particularly if they are used as though the numbers are the actual facts. Here is why. As discussed previously, many of the components of customer profitability interact and there is no way to measure that interaction. Also, many of the activities that influence the profitability of the customer, such as what I like to call the "PITA" factor (I suggest "pain" for the P, you make up the rest.), just can't be measured.

One might then say, "then how am I to determine which customer is which?" My response is that you can do a great deal of good by dealing with extremes. Most profit centers have BSL's they can identify from a mile away and address. They also have CC's that can easily be identified and taken care of properly. It is safe to generally conclude the rest are currently CP's, where attention needs to be focused on how you are doing business, not whether you are doing business. This is not to say there aren't measurements you can use. For example, a customer that has an overall margin of 10% and pays in 120 days is not making you any money. Just don't rely on your equations in an absolute fashion.

Let's look at some specific things that you might do with the different types of customers, once you have a general idea what category they are in:

Cash Cows

This category of customer looks deceptively simple to deal with at first. One's first reaction would be to simply keep taking orders and banking the money. When that is the strategy, trouble lurks in the future. Remember, a CC usually pays the bills (your bills) and makes all of the profit in the profit center and then some. They are probably a good fit with the profit center's market focus and quite often can have healthy margins. In just those two sentences, here are the problems that can arise if we have no strategy other than to keep taking orders:

- Since the profitability of the profit center lies in the future viability of the relationship with the CC's, every effort must be made to not lose them and even improve your position if at all possible. This would mean that every day, your profit center must be the best supplier that there is for that customer. The profit center manager needs to maintain contact with the CC to ensure that customer care evolves as the CC's needs for care evolve. With the efficiency that is usually associated with dealing with a CC, that shouldn't be too hard to do *unless* you let a BSL get in the way. How can a BSL ruin a relationship with a CC and hamper the quality of service? Easy. Is your delivery truck available to service the CC while it is going to the job site of the BSL for the third time to explain to them that what you delivered is what they ordered? No. Is your inside salesman available to take that CC's phone call while he is on the phone with the BSL listening to him rant? No. Even worse is the more systematic self-defeat of changing your business and value/service offering to better serve the BSL at the expense of the CC. An example would be changing from a premier line of fittings that the CC's prefer because with that line you aren't competitive enough at the BSL.

- Be aware that if a customer is a CC for no other reason except for the fact that you are able to price material at an unusually "healthy" margin, this business may be vulnerable. High margins without a superior value offering must be dealt with delicately. What if in order to keep the business you had to lower those extraordinary margins? Would this customer still be a CC? What if that customer is your only CC and the reason you have the customer is because the customer has not decided or had time to change suppliers, yet? You are in a pickle! In this case, your entire strategy for success is to hope that your competition doesn't ever figure out how to deal you a deathblow, and hope is a pretty unreliable strategy. In the section on "sales strategy mistakes", you will discover that one of the reasons discussed for writing business is "because you haven't lost it yet." If you take that article to heart, you probably want to make sure that with the CC, you have a superior value/service offering. Unfortunately, (or luckily, depending on which side you are on), almost all distributors have business simply because someone hasn't taken it from them yet. The customer would welcome another supplier if they thought there was one out there--they just don't think there is.

A real life example of this is that industrial MRO customer that just sends you orders and you deliver them and charge the customer whatever you wish. Then one day the competition comes in and offers the customer a strategic sourcing agreement with all the associated bells and whistles and WHAM! You just lost a CC. For more discussion, see the articles on "Why PCM's Should Call on Customers", "Customer Service", and "Sales Strategy Mistakes."

Maintaining Cash Cows

To avoid these pitfalls, the following are a few things that you want to make sure that you are doing with your CC's.

- Ensure that your relationship with the customer is second to none. Know from the customer's perspective, that they are happy with your profit center. A solid relationship will help you to learn early on of any competitive threats. *Accomplishing this involves direct PC Management involvement.*
- Make sure everyone in the profit center knows who the CC's are and the service (extra effort) level that they require. Also, make sure that your employees know not to allow the needs of BSL's to undermine the service that they give to the CC's.
- Here is an idea (not mine). What if you went through your customer list and rated your customers by profitability then came up with some method to identify them (like one, two or three asterisks in the customer heading), to indicate a customer's profitability in CEDNet. By doing this, every employee can know a customer's ranking just by looking that customer up in the order entry screen. Then, suppose one of the three asterisk (CC) customers call up and needs something that will require "extra effort", such as running a

part that the customer left off of an order out to a jobsite right away. That person who took the phone call instantly knows to tell the customer that he will drop everything and take it out to him personally right then.

- Be sure that everything about how you run your profit center is built to serve the CC's.
- Closely related to the above bullet, don't build your business on input from anywhere other than the input of your CC's. If a CC asks you to stock a new product, then do (and I am pretty close to saying "no matter what" here). If a vendor comes in with some fancy gizmo that he wants you to buy a recommended stock of and put on display at the counter—don't. A sure sign of a distributor that hasn't figured out the concept of market focus and customer selection is when that distributor makes decisions on stocking new products and changing lines based on vendor input or anything other than what CC's ask.
- Always make sure that you are doing everything possible to further improve your position at CC's to reduce competitive threats.
- Make sure that your best people have responsibility for handling the business of the CC's and that they are not bothered with the BSL's. Assign the "C" players to service the BSL's until the time comes that you decide to rid yourself of both.

- Always have a plan to pursue the right number (which might be one) of new CC's. You don't want to have all of your future profitability rest in the hands of one or two CC's--particularly if you are in a defenseless position relative to price. If you are thinking in terms of customer profitability, you will get a feel for identifying which customers are profitable and which are not. Use this feel when pursuing new customers and only pursue those that have a reasonable chance of becoming a CC.
- Last, but not least, never let your success with a CC rest in the hands of one or two people in your profit center. The worst-case scenario would be to have a generally poor service model and rely on the extra effort of an outside salesman to maintain the business. This situation places your profit center in a very vulnerable position.

The math of customer profitability

Before moving on to BSL's and CP's, let's talk about the interaction of the three customer types relative to time. It is arguable that the more GP one can generate in a given amount of time, (as in man/hours), the better the chance of making a bottom line profit. It is also arguable that, by definition, one could generate more GP in a given amount of time with a CC than with a BSL. To put relative numbers on it, if the average customer takes 1 unit of time to generate 1 unit of profit, a CC would take about 1/2 of a unit of time to generate 1 unit of profit. So the distributor that has a CC will either generate 2 units of profit in that 1 unit of time, or it might decide to generate the one unit of profit with 1/2 a unit of time and use the other half a unit of time to pursue another CC and make sure the existing CC is happy, or some combination of both.

A BSL, on the other hand takes 2 units of time to generate the same 1 unit of GP. There are many problems with that. First, since we can only afford to spend 1 unit of time, the second unit amounts to losses. Second, since we are only able to afford 1 unit of time, we won't have the time available to properly serve the BSL, improve position at the CP, or go find a CC. What this looks like in real life is everyone in the profit center is working their tails off, yet no one is making any money!

Even if that profit center found a CC, they would never secure and maintain the business because we are wasting so much time with the BSL. Continuing on with the math, every time a distributor can identify and eliminate a BSL and replace it with a CC, he trades in 2x work for 1/2x work. That sends the expense of 1-1/2x work straight to the bottom line!

Hold on, it gets even better!

That BSL is now going to go buy from the competition. Now *they* spend 2x amount of work for every 1x of GP. That extra "x" of work causes the competition to drop the ball with their CC. Since we got rid of the BSL, we have 1-1/2x extra capacity, which of course we use to secure the business from the CC, of the competition.

Once the concept of customer profitability is understood by a distributor in a market, it starts a chain reaction where the rich get richer and the poor get poorer. If your profit center is in a situation where you just can't keep up, yet you need to lower your expenses, you are most certainly straddled with too many BSL's. And when you look at profit centers that can't seem to help but make money and do so without a lot of effort, (and you want to keep telling yourself that they must have an easier market, or some kind of special situation), it is probably because they have a high amount of CC's relative to BSL's.

Beauty is in the eyes of the beholder

One more thought on Market Focus. A CC is only a CC to those distributors that are set up to serve the CC's customer type well and efficiently. This example illustrates the point. Let's say that in a market, there is a "flower buying" CC and a "bulk oil buying" CC. Only a distributor set up to sell flowers will experience the profits from the flower customer and likewise for the bulk oil customers.

This may sound extreme, but I don't think it is all that different from what we often do. I know of a profit center that had chosen a market focus of small contractors in the nearby vicinity that often come to the counter to pick material up. Makes good enough sense, doesn't it? It would also follow that this target customer base would be where all of the CC's would exist for that profit center. But, you go look at the profit center and what you see is a lighting specialist, a gear specialist and an inside sales person. Every time someone comes in to the counter it looks like what you would expect to see if someone went into Saks Fifth Avenue and ordered a hamburger. There are no processes in place to handle will-call orders so every time one occurred it was a new adventure. The profit center had chosen flower customers as their CC's, but built their business to serve the bulk oil customers. The lesson is you will make your money with the customer type that you choose to build your business around.

Blood Sucking Losers

As mentioned earlier, a BSL's claim to fame is that they not only lose lots of money, but they actually hamper or eliminate a profit center's ability to retain CC's. It is easy to get too narrow a focus on what BSL's are and think that BSL's are those awful, cheap, customers that don't know how to run their business. There are many ways for a customer to be a BSL. They can be too far away. They can have needs that don't fit the services you provide. Or there can simply be too much competition for the customer to make a fair profit (or the competition can just be too good). These are some of the ways either singularly or more commonly in combinations that can make a customer a BSL.

Another important characteristic of a BSL is that expenses remain typically a set percentage of sales or gross profit. So if selling a dollar loses you twenty cents, then selling a million dollars will lose you $200,000. So don't wait for business to "pick up" if you are saddled with a crop of BSL's-- life won't get better, it will get worse.

How to rid yourself of BSL's—easily

These customers must be identified and eliminated. Here are a few ideas on how to do that:

- Raise the **price**. There is a price at which any customer is profitable. Does that mean that all of your BSL's can be made profitable? Probably not. In many cases the price that you would need to charge to make a profit is well above what the market would allow. There is, however, usually room to move up on price and retain a profitable portion of the business. or mitigate your losses. An example would be a BSL that is constantly sending out quotes for miscellaneous bills of material and also buys material at your counter for whatever price you charge. By deciding to **stop quoting**, you could give up that BSL part of the business and retain the CC counter business. You know how you have that pricing conversation with your inside salespeople and you hear them talk about how they don't want to gouge the customer. Hey, I can understand that. I can also understand that if you have a BSL, that would be a perfect place for the inside sales people to gouge the customer.

- You can use **credit**. I hate to count how many times I have seen a profit center with a BSL that doesn't pay within terms and we find ourselves thinking we are doing that profit center a favor by "finding a way" to continue selling the customer. It is not a favor.

- Don't **assign a salesman to the account**. That usually has the double impact of lowering the amount of (BSL) business that we do, as well as lowering the cost of serving because there is no OS function to pay for, not to mention the fact that the salesman will now have more time available to find some CC's. ***If you pick only one thing to do to improve in the area of customer selection, it probably ought to be making sure that you don't deploy outside salesmen to call on BSL's, or worse yet, pay them commission to bring that (agonizing) business in the door.***

- More complicated, but still important techniques revolve around how resources are allocated. Don't stock material just for a BSL, don't allocate service resources for a BSL. Don't make decisions on how to run your business because of a BSL. Only do things that are good for you and your CC's.

By now, I hope you are thinking of who your CC's and BSL's are and thinking about how you can reallocate resources from the BSL's to the CC's with the long term hope of getting rid of BSL's all together. But we still haven't covered what is usually the biggest part of your customer base--the Conditionally/Marginally Profitable customers (CP's).

Conditionally/Marginally Profitable Customers

CP's are basically CC's or BSL's with a few exceptions. There are usually one or two things about a CP that keeps it from being in one of the other categories. Your job is to identify the CP and determine what the one or two things are. While you are always looking for ways to keep CC's and lose BSL's, with CP's you are looking to *change* the relationship. The most common differentiator for a CP is account position. If you are pursuing a very large contractor for example, it would almost always be a CP. For the distributor that is in the #1 position, it is a CC, for everyone else it is a marginal loser to a BSL. *Because of this, conventional thinking would tell you that you would never want to pursue many large, CP customers at once. By doing so, you lock yourself into the #2 or #3 position at all of the accounts, guaranteeing that you will lose money with all of them.* A better approach would be to choose just one of those large contractors and do everything possible to get in the #1 position as quickly as possible. Remember that you will be losing money on the account until you do.

Here is an example of the difference in profitability between being #1 and #3. Let's say there is a customer that buys 50 -2-1/2″ connectors per week. If you are the #1 supplier and are in the position of getting the order as long as you have the product, then you stock 100 and have 12 turns with a 100% fill rate. If you are the #3 supplier, you will have 8 on the shelf that are in writedown status until you get that once-every-four-years call for 50. At that point you sell 8 and unimpress the customer yet again. When I am given the opportunity to go into a profit center and evaluate the possible reasons for a lack of profitability, one of the first things that I typically do is review the sales registers to see the product content. If they are made up of things such as a disconnect, pipe and wire, some wire connectors and conduit fittings, that's good. If the orders consist of the hub for a disconnect, one crimp lug and a 2-1/2″ two hole strap, that's bad. In the first case the profit center is the primary supplier for that customer and in the second case, the fill in supplier.

Another way the difference between being #1 and anything else can manifest itself is on fixture and gear jobs if you're in that business. When you talk to a profit center manager that generally is in the number one position with his customers about fixture and gear jobs, you will hear him talk in terms of getting last look and all the interplay in writing orders with a reasonable level of profitability. Talk to one that isn't in that position and all you hear about is how competitive the market is. Funny, isn't it? All the distributors that are not in the top position are in more competitive markets than the ones that are.

To further clarify the previous point, the #1 position with the customer might not mean having the most sales to that customer. Your goal should be to be the *preferred* distributor for selling what it is that you want to sell. So if your preference is to sell load centers via delivery and at the counter, but not to do big lighting jobs, then your goal should be to dominate that business. The key is to be in a position to get the business that you want with very little effort or expense and you aren't going to get that by being second choice. In other words, you want to be the "first call."

So what if you are second choice and there is little hope today of being first choice? Because you have become a student of customer selection and customer profitability, you are aware that you will typically lose money in the #2 position at a CP customer. You have an important decision to make. On the one hand, being number two almost guarantees that you will lose money with a CP. On the other, that is the position that you must to be in if you ever hope to be number one. There is a lot to be said for having a strategy of being a strong #2 and waiting for the #1 guy to drop the ball.

Often times, the profitability of the CP is dependant on one factor. It could be how you handle the customer from a credit standpoint, or the price you charge. It can even be the transaction itself. Maybe it is the way the customer is dealing with you that makes him unprofitable--so you need to change the transaction process, if possible. Unlike the BSL, however, you are not tweaking these parameters of the relationship to rid yourself of the customer. The tweaking is done to go from losing money to making money.

Account Assignment and CP's

A very important "tweak" that can be used with CP's involves account position and account assignments. If an outside salesman's account package includes five CP customers where the profit center's low share makes those customers unprofitable, you could remove some of the accounts so that the salesman can focus on getting into a dominant position at only a few of the accounts. If that doesn't work, then you further reduce the number of CP's assigned until the number is one. This has a twofold effect. *First, the penetration of the accounts that remain assigned goes up, thereby improving profitability. Second, the less profitable sales to the accounts that are unassigned go down.*

Before I close this thing out, there are a few miscellaneous points that I would like to make.

- You can select a customer or a part of a customer. You don't have to choose customers in whole increments. You can choose to do their daily business, but not pursue the bid/job business, or visa versa. You can choose to pursue the field foreman, but not purchasing. You can even choose to pursue certain products, but not others.

- Customer selection, market focus, and customer service all go together. And they don't have to go together in any particular order. You can choose profitable customers in your account base and then choose to focus on those customers and others like them. Or you can choose a market and then begin to select customers that are profitable in that segment. Another way is to see what you are good at, i.e., where you provide the best service and make that customer base your focus, etc., etc. In the end, you want to have a targeted market, profitable customers within that market that you pursue in some sort of organized fashion, and a value/service offering that is important to those customers.

The impact of commissions on customer profitability

Once you really understand the concept of customer profitability, you will quickly see that commissioned salesmen and maximizing customer profitability don't really go together--*at all.* A straight commission outside salesman isn't paid any less to bring in unprofitable business than to bring in profitable business. Nor is a commissioned salesman paid more to make sure that the business that you are doing is as profitable as it can be. If you are in a situation where your salesmen are on commission and you don't choose to change that anytime soon, then this entire article becomes that much more important to you. Several things become much more important to you (not that they aren't important to others). A keen awareness of customer profitability must be used in concert with an active role in salesmen account assignments. So you don't assign BSL's at all and you only assign CP's one or two at a time. The worst thing you can do is have a salesman on straight commission and give him a large number of big (as in most likely to be CP's or BSL's) accounts. Your agreement with a salesman should be that it is his responsibility to turn the CP's into CC's if he wants to keep them or get more. An even worse situation is to allow that salesman to keep any BSL's. It is crucial in order to have an effective account assignment strategy, utilizing commissioned outside salesmen, that the PC manager is in *direct* contact with the customer. Why? It just doesn't make sense to rely on a commissioned outside salesmen for information on the potential profitability of a customer. If the customer could be a CC, but appears to us to be a BSL because of poor coverage, is the salesman going to volunteer that it is his entire fault? I don't think so! His job is to get and keep accounts and continue to get paid commission.

Customer selection and profit center size

Though I am writing only one article on customer selection, how well one does in this area manifests itself very differently depending on the size of the profit center. I haven't used an analogy in a few pages, so here goes one. In this analogy, I will use bodies of water to represent profit centers and nuclear waste to represent unprofitable customers. First the small profit center example. If you had a small body of water, like a bathtub and you put one teaspoon of nuclear waste in it, you have ruined the bath. No bath tonight and no hope of one until you tear out the bathtub and get a new one, plus have some hazmat guys come by to visit--but no big deal. Once you get the new bathtub, you are ready to go.

For the big profit center example let's consider the Atlantic Ocean. You could probably pour a couple of tons of hazardous waste into the Atlantic per day for quite a while before it was even measurable. 100 tons of hazardous waste and people would still be swimming in the ocean. So which situation is better, the bathtub or the ocean? At first, it seems like the ocean. But once the tonnage of hazardous waste gets to a detectable level, what do you have? You can't just change the ocean out. Way too much damage has been done. The fish are all dead. The entire ecosystem of the earth is out of balance.

The point is, that in a small profit center, poor customer selection habits can be a quick knock-out blow, annihilating all hope of profitability with only a few (or possibly even one) of the wrong customers. But once the problem is recognized, it is fixed easily. In a larger profit center, the good news and bad news is that it is more resilient to customer selection errors. It can make 200x in profit and waste 120x on BSL's and not look too bad because it has 80x left. But when you finally realize what the problem is, the solution will be very complex and take a long time to fix, if it even can be fixed. There can be commissioned outside salesmen making huge amounts of money, but a lot of it is with BSL's and CP's. You want to restructure the account packages, but that is pretty sensitive. There could even be entire departments built around BSL's (data department, that industrial initiative, etc.). Like the Atlantic, this is a far bigger problem than that bathtub. I think the point is that, though the customer selection problem will manifest itself differently, it is of paramount importance no matter what the size of the profit center or the level of profitability.

You might be thinking that you know of examples where a particular distributor is highly profitable, but doesn't seem to be very astute in the customer selection, market focus arena. That leads you to wonder if this entire article is wrong. *It is not.* Usually when this is the case, it is because the competitive landscape is such that it is relatively easy to make money on many customers and many types of customers, probably because no distributor is very good and all have a weak value/service offering. In that case, if one distributor chose to pick a market area to focus on, chose the most profitable customers in that market, and then get good at serving those customers, the landscape would change dramatically (remember the whole 1/2x, 2x discussion). And eventually, someone will do that.

This entire discussion can play out in many different ways, depending on your market, the size of your profit center, and the competitive landscape. The key is to buy in to the concept, come up with a method to determine which customer is which from a profitability standpoint, let your people know which customer is which, and build your business around those customers. Then stop pursuing BSL's and get rid of them when you can.

FOCUS AND CUSTOMER SELECTION...GETTING THE TEAM IN THE BOAT

Once you develop an understanding of the concept of market focus and customer selection and have begun to develop an idea of where you want to take the business, you must find a way to get the rest of the team on board with you. This process isn't all that easy, because these concepts go against most people's instinct that all gross profit is good. The following are a few suggestions on how to make some progress with the team.

1. As is discussed in the market focus article, make sure that your employees and suppliers know exactly what your market focus is and why. They can't support you unless they know what you want them to support them with.

2. When it comes to customer selection, take the time to show your employees how they are losing money by dealing with unprofitable customers. Make sure they understand the concept that by dealing with a BSL, they are unavailable to serve a CC. Have a way to make sure that all employees know who the CC's, CP's, and BSL's are and that all customers should not be treated equally.

3. Don't assign an account to an outside salesman that is outside of your focus and un-assign any accounts that had been previously assigned. Do the same with unprofitable customers. If a customer starts looking like they are a BSL, engage in conversations early with the OS to create an awareness that the current business relationship cannot continue. This allows time to correct the situation if that is possible.

4. Make sure that everyone in the profit center understands that there are a lot of good reasons to not respond to a request for quote. Create a mentality that you don't do something just because it came across the fax.

5. Make sure that credit is on board with you. You don't want credit thinking that they are doing you a favor by finding ways to sell a customer that is unprofitable in the end anyway.

6. Lead by example. Spend your time improving your profit center as it relates to your chosen customers in your chosen focus. Make line decisions based on what your chosen customers want. Put your capacity where your best customers need it.

CAPACITY

This little, unassuming term—capacity (as in your profit center's capacity) has an impact on your profit center that is significant enough that I thought it deserved its own article. The impact is that it determines *how much you can sell.* This article is a follow up to the others, most notably the ones on customer selection and market focus, so if you haven't read those yet, you might want to as they will be referred to in this article.

Capacity has global components.

- How much you spend. All things being equal, the more you spend, the more capacity you have. Of course, this costs more.

- How effective you are at using the resources that you bought. That includes processes, motivation, balance, and waste. Effectiveness determines how much capacity you have, relative to how much you spend.

Customer selection and market focus don't change capacity. However, they are very closely related. If a normal capacity is X, a high capacity might be 1.5x. Focus and customer selection won't raise that number any higher. The impact of customer selection and market focus is that they require less capacity to serve, thereby increasing sales and profitability. So, if you have 1.5x and you sell to all CC's (remember that a CC only takes 0.5x effort, or capacity to serve), then you can now sell 3x potentially, while only paying for 1.5X, making you very profitable.

The definition of capacity

Let me propose to you the concept of capacity that we will cover. I am doing this early in the game, because I think most people will come up with a lot of arguments to the concept right away. Thinking of those arguments will help you think about the impact of capacity. So here it is:

If capacity is defined as "X" number of normal employees that are normally motivated, normally skilled, and normally equipped, then a profit center with "X" employees will sell "X" electrical supplies over the long haul to the customer base that it is built to serve, as long as there is enough available market.

You should have questions already, like "So what the heck are my outside salesmen doing all day?" or "Yeah, but what if I write this $300k wire order that I am quoting today? Won't that change the laws of the universe?" or "You mean to tell me that if all distributors had the same amount of employees, they would all do the same amount of business?"

Now that I wrote the concept, I realize that there is a little room to explain. First of all, normal is as in *average*. The term "equipped" means the tools to do the job, properly applied. So a truck driver with a truck would have more capacity than a truck driver without a truck. For that matter, a truck driver with two trucks wouldn't have any more capacity than one with one truck. And of course, a truck driver with a truck that works will have more capacity than a truck driver with a truck that is broke.

Normally equipped refers to how the tools are used. Obviously, a back order tub is a backorder tub, but it can be used in many different ways. This refers to *processes*.

Inventory is a tool (a big one).

"Over the long haul" refers to an average over the years.

So yes, go ahead and write your wire order. But if you write a $300k wire order every day of the year, your business will not grow incrementally by that amount over the long haul unless you add the right amount of "X" capacity to handle that wire order. "Over the long haul" also implies that you can run at 1.1X or 1.2X for a short time without losing any business. This is an important concept.

"Electrical supplies" is measured in sales *effort*, not GP (remember the 1/2X and 2x customers). And of course, the reference to "available market" makes the point that you can only get as much business as the marketplace can offer.

As it stands right now in the discussion, you have Xne (normal employees) = Xb (business) and as a result, the profit your Xb minus the cost of your Xne equals a normal amount of profit (Xp). So we have a bunch of normal profit centers making normal profit with normal people selling normal stuff. It's sort of like the Edward Scissorhands movie.

Let's look at how we can change the equation, because in reality, instead of being the simple one above, it's about 8 inches long.

First, we will change those normal employees (Xne):

Motivation (M)-If you can get "X" productivity out of a normally motivated employee, then you can get more or less (maybe from 0.5X to 1.5X) depending on how they are motivated. This usually gives CED a leg up on our competition because our business model, properly applied, is more motivating than most others.

Skill and Ability (S)-Obviously, if a normally skilled employee can produce "X", then a smarter, more experienced, one will produce more. This highlights the importance of training and the importance of hanging onto the "A" players in your profit center.

Tools (T)-This can be changed in many ways, but an example would be that if someone was making wire cuts with a hand crank wire machine, they would not produce as much as someone using an electric wire machine. Or an inside salesperson with all the inventory they need will perform better than an employee that has something less than that.

Processes (P)- Processes are notable because they can be exchanged for "extra effort", or used together with extra effort. This flexibility gives processes a little added importance. If your capacity is partly the sum of your employees' motivation (extra effort) and the effectiveness of your processes, and you want to increase your capacity, it is easier and quicker to increase the motivation part of the equation. To put it another way, if you determine that you to need to increase your capacity beyond normal for a short while, which would you rather do; tell your employees "Guys, we are going to have to really kick it in over this next month with all the business we are getting," or re-write and implement new order processing practices?

Motivation, Tools, and Processes all together and they go together more than you think

Maybe you are thinking, "This stuff looks like too much work...I am just going to get some great employees and motivate the heck out of them. They will just make all this stuff work out." From what I remember from my studies of people like Edward Demming, I can tell you that such a solution is over simplistic. That is because the tools to do the job and the processes to make it work correctly have the characteristic of being management's responsibility. Let's take that highly motivated employee that is going to make everything work out OK for you by being highly motivated. Send him out to make a bunch of wire cuts on that 1920 wire machine that broke 40 years ago and what does he think? Is he saying, "I guess I am going to kick in some extra effort here to make all of this work." No. He is going to say, "management doesn't care whether this gets done, so why should I?" Same thing for no inventory, no trucks and everything else. *The best way to have a motivated crew is to show them by your actions that you care whether they have the tools to get their job done.*

Value/Service Offering (Vso)-Closely related to customer service, the Vso refers to doing things that make you more valuable to the customer and, as a result, make doing business with that customer easier on him and you. In the article on customer selection, we talked about how being the first call, or the preferred supplier particularly with a "CP" customer made life much easier even to point of making the difference between profitability and non-profitability. This is that same subject. So increasing your "Vso" increases your capacity.

Next in the equation, we change the amount of gross profit we make:

Gross Profit Percentage (GP)-You know this, so I won't go into it. The only point that I will make is that, once you see that you only have so much capacity to sell, making more gross profit per sales dollar becomes that much more important. That is why you will see a "higher profit" profit center have a greater tendency to turn down orders. They know if they take that wire order at 15% that has 60 cuts, that it will take away from their capacity to handle wire orders from other, more profitable customers. To be technically correct, I should point out that GP doesn't really change capacity (as defined as sales effort), but it does change the money you make for any given amount of sales effort.

At this point you can come up with a mental concept of how to calculate your capacity. The equation looks like this:

Capacity=X (number of employees)(M x S x T x P x Vso)

If an average amount of each of the items above is one, then a profit center that had an average amount of every ingredient would have a capacity equation that looked something like: Xne (number of normal employees) x 1 x 1 x 1 etc., with each of those 1's representing an ingredient of capacity. But in real life, each one is not average, so the equation looks like this: X (1.1 x 1.2 x 0.8 x 0.4 etc.)

Where are all of my outside salesmen?????

So far in this article, we have basically made the point that whatever your capacity is, that is about how much you will sell. If you are above capacity, over time you will lose business and visa versa. So what do these outside salesmen do? Why do you even have them?

An outside salesman operating in the pure form of selling, i.e., asking for business, does not change capacity and, therefore, does not increase business beyond your existing capacity. If you have a profit center with 10 employees, one of whom is an outside salesman and your profit center is operating at full capacity, then you add another outside salesman, your business will probably not grow. I know that is highly controversial and many of you are thinking of perfect examples of real-life exceptions. I will describe those exceptions.

If you have a really good outside salesman, he will make part of his job improving the processes (P), and increasing value (Vso). He should also be increasing customer profitability by getting more "CC's", and improving penetration into "CP's" --in other words, finding business that requires less capacity to serve. **So this salesman really is increasing sales**, but he is doing so by increasing capacity and getting business that needs less capacity to serve.

That is ***entirely*** different than that salesman that has been recently deployed to go call on 40 accounts in a remote area with no change in the profit center's capacity. That plan has backfire written all over it because, instead of growing the business, those activities are sucking resources (capacity) away from what are probably some profitable customers.

Many times, the outside salesman is not operating in the pure form of selling all the time. So if that salesman is operating as a pure outside salesman 20% of the time and adding capacity 80% of the time (doing quotes, making deliveries, doing inside sales work), then your business will grow by the amount of capacity that salesman added (in this case, 0.8X). This explains why it is effective to take an existing inside salesman that you want to move into outside sales and give him only 0.1x outside sales responsibility, i.e., one account. It also explains why taking an existing inside salesman and putting him on the road full time is a "plan" (see above) that is doomed. *It is doomed because it involves simultaneously reducing capacity while trying to increase sales.* Salesman may not add business, but they will shift capacity!

If the outside salesman is actually selling all the time, he will get business. No salesman has ever gone "0"-fer (somebody tell me how to spell this—Gates didn't know). But I will bet you that the overall sales of the profit center won't change. Before the additional outside salesman came along, you were selling 10x. The first outside salesman was doing 6x and the house was doing 4x. Now the second salesman comes along and he is doing 2x. The first salesman and the house are now doing 8x combined. Because there was no additional capacity, the salesman #2 just took capacity from salesman #1. Think of it this way, how many people can an inside salesperson talk to at once? *There is a universal law (I think there is, or at least there should be) that doing any given thing most certainly guarantees that you won't be doing something else.*

What if that second salesman starts calling on BSL's? With the whole 1/2x-2x dynamic, he could reduce sales by sucking resources from efficient CC's and reallocating those resources into marginal or loser accounts. The lesson that is very important to understand is that account assignments are extremely important—particularly with a new salesman.

One way that your business can grow with that second outside salesman is if you really weren't operating at full capacity. That is why it typically makes more sense for a large profit center to add an outside salesman because they would most likely have additional capacity.

Another way that an outside salesman can increase business is by taking the profit center over capacity. Remember how we talked earlier about how a profit center could go at 1.2X capacity for a short while, but over the long haul your business will go down to X? It is feasible that an outside salesman could run the sales up to 1.2X of capacity then the profit center could increase capacity to fill the shortfall. So maybe the outside salesman increases sales by adding some "CC's" and then the profit center increases capacity by getting rid of some "BSL's". Even without increasing capacity, an outside salesman, using the power of relationships, should be able to allow a profit center to operate at a higher percentage of its capacity than it might otherwise. But remember, that might mean that he can change it from .8X to .95X, but he won't eliminate the limiting factor that you aren't going to sell much more than X for very long.

The point of all the previous discussion is not that outside salesmen don't grow the business, but it is very important to understand that a profit center will not sell anymore than it has the capacity to sell. So a profit center that is over capacity (meaning that it is operating beyond its capacity) because it is selling to too many BSL's won't grow its business by adding an outside salesman. That is why we almost never (almost because of some of the exceptions noted above) see a profit center that is losing money hire an outside salesman and grow into profitability. If I had to distill this entire discussion on capacity and its relation to the outside selling function, it would be this:

You should never have any more outside selling effort than you have capacity.

To put one final point on it, here is an example of a profit center that I see regularly:

- If you go into the profit center and look around, you can tell that it is operating way over its capacity. The counterman's job seems to be to tell customers what they don't have in stock today, and the inside salesman's job seems to be to tell customers that they don't have a truck available. Blatant examples of operating over the profit center's capacity.

- This profit center has two outside salesman running around town and I don't really know what they are doing. However I do know that they aren't spending time improving processes because they don't seem to interface with the profit center much.
- The profit center spends some 25% of its GP on the outside sales function.
- The profit center is losing money and hasn't grown for a long time (it seems to be getting impacted by the down economy more than others).
- The profit center manager thinks that his business is going to grow to a point where someday, he will make a profit.

In fact, it is going to get worse. Since a long-term customer tends to be more profitable than a new one, the outside function will only serve to bring in new business that drives the profit center that much more beyond its capacity, causing the existing customers to flee that much faster.

One side note. Since I have beat up on the value of outside salesmen quite a bit here, I feel like I should defend them a little in the name of capacity. You know how most red-blooded outside salesmen have it in their genetic make up to use the phrases "we never have anything in stock" and "I never get any inside support?" More often than you think, they are right!

Operating beyond your capacity

Another point that I would expect many to argue is the point that you can't operate over capacity over the long haul. I could see how one might say that that is what they are supposed to do—that it is an indication of operating efficiently, i.e., having a high GP per employee. I am not saying that every time you find yourself making a lot of money you should hire another employee. But in some cases, you should. An even safer bet is to always be looking at the cheaper ways to raise capacity, like improving processes, the quality of your team and the quality of your customer base.

Here is what I am talking about. Let's say that you are in a market and you are the only supply house in that market and you are really good. You have excellence in every area of the profit center. Your customers love you. You have 10X capacity and are doing 15X business, making you wildly profitable.

Now, let's say that a competitor comes to town and opens up across the street. Every aspect of their supply house is only mediocre. They bring no special value to the customer base. Their value proposition is something like, "give us a shot". On day one, they get no business. On day thirty, they get no business. But eventually, some customer is going to wonder why he continues to wait for thirty minutes at your counter, which is operating at maximum capacity, when there seems to be no waiting across the street. He starts thinking, I don't care how good CED is or how bad the other guy is, surely they can fill this simple order. Then a customer calls your super-great inside person, also over capacity, that he loves. How many times does he hold on the phone before he finally hangs up and calls the bad guys? Eventually, your business will go down to 10X and theirs will go up to 5X.

This phenomenon explains why you might often get advice from an experienced manager to not take that really big order that you want to book. Here is a quiz. If you are a $4 million dollar profit center (operating at capacity) and you get a $3 million dollar per year piece of business that will last 3 years, how much business will you now be doing? How much business will you be doing at the end of the three years? The answer is not $7 million and then back to $4 million. You would likely go up to $5 million and then down to $2 million when the project is over. Capacity kicks in.

Your might be thinking that you are operating well beyond your capacity as you read this and that things are going just fine. In the article on sales strategy mistakes, you saw that one of the reasons presented about why we get orders is because we haven't lost them yet. In other words, we deserve to lose the business—and we will. The customer just hasn't found the right alternative supplier yet. And if you are thinking that the right alternative doesn't exist, the ways of the capitalistic society that we live in would deem that it will exist soon.

Balance – the key to capacity

Here is another quiz:

- If a profit center has $7 million dollars in inventory, 20 inside salespeople, 10 outside people, twenty delivery trucks, and one phone line, how many orders can inside sales take at one time?
- If a profit center has 4 delivery trucks and one driver, how many deliveries can it make at once?
- If your only delivery vehicle is a 25-foot stake body that gets 4 mpg and your only order to be delivered is one 30-amp fuse, how many fuses will you deliver?

The key to balance is to have as many resources of any given type that you need, and no more. When we are talking about all of these equations, we are only talking about the needed capacity. Everything else is just waste. So when you put together your 8-inch long equation, at the end will be "minus waste (W)." In other words, it is over simplistic to say that the more resources you have, the more you will sell. It has to be the right resources.

If waste is one component that determines balance, a bottleneck is the other. You can think of this as a water pipe (your capacity) with water flowing through it at a constant pressure (that's the business). If you started with a 2″ diameter pipe with a certain amount of pressure, it would flow a certain amount of water. That would be a perfectly balanced situation. Now, let's take the middle part of that pipe and replace it with 6″ pipe and leave the ends at 2″. What is its capacity now? No change. The 6″ section is just waste. Now let's take the 6″ section out and replace it with a 1″ section. The capacity is now that of a 1″ pipe. The 1″ pipe is a bottleneck.

I would think that a good manager would spend his entire working life looking for the bottlenecks and waste and fixing them. I would also think that a profit center manager reading some of the preceding pages might be thinking, "This is much more complicated than what I signed up for." In reality, the way the subject of balance plays out is like this. In the normal, day to day, process of running the profit center and interacting with all of the various areas that make up the capacity of the profit center, the profit center manager should get a *feel* for where the bottlenecks are and where the waste is. As he is managing the profit center he is always trying to fix both, or at least not make the situation worse. That might mean actually buying and selling things or hiring and firing people. Or it could just mean nudging resources in one direction or the other. If you are over capacity in purchasing and under capacity in inside sales, but inside sales has historically done the purchasing on their own specials, then you might shift that duty to purchasing.

Some final takeaways from this discussion

- If you think that you are operating beyond your current capacity, don't think that additional outside sales activity will fix your problem.
- Look at the components of capacity and balance. More than likely, there are ways to increase your capacity without spending any money.
- Evaluate your capacity from the bottom up. First you need inventory, then you need a way to get it to your customer, then you need someone to take the order, then you need people to get the customer to give you the order. You wouldn't want to be short on inventory and have too many outside salesmen, as an example.
- Unprofitable (BSL) customers have a bigger impact on your effective capacity than you think. As said before, a BSL doesn't change capacity, but because of the amount of available resources it takes to serve, it leaves less capacity for the good customers.
- Don't let yourself get caught thinking that any one aspect of capacity will overcome all other shortfalls. In other words, don't think that you can "motivate" your way through all other problems.

- Without doing a lot of evaluation, if your profit center is not making the kind of money that it should, it is probably overpaying for the outside sales function.
- Balance determines how efficient your capacity will be.

Like all the other discussion topics in these articles, this one on capacity is not meant to say that capacity is the sum total of everything that impacts your business. There are still a lot of things that can determine your final profitability (like vendor relations, as an example). On the other hand, capacity is similar to the other subjects in that it has a far bigger impact on your profitability than you might think and a thorough knowledge and awareness of the subject might help to point out why some things just never seem to get better no matter what you do.

THE RELATIONSHIP BETWEEN MARKET FOCUS AND CAPACITY

I know you are thinking about the "D" cell batteries in the Beijing story (from the focus article), and you think to yourself, "I just don't see how in the world the local Home Depot down the street from me could take every product out of their store except the "D" cell batteries and become more profitable in the process. You are probably thinking the same thing about your Profit Center. Let me try to clarify the subject. It has to do with *capacity*.

Think about the concept that for an electrical distributor built a certain way, there is a particular market that is the most profitable. If one market is more profitable than others, then doing a lot of business in that market would be the best option.

To do a lot of business in that particular segment, you would need to be good enough to beat most of the competition most of the time, and it is arguable that you will not succeed at getting good at a lot of things, so you should focus on only a few (or one).

Given 10X capacity, you would want to get really good at serving your chosen type of X's, then you would go out and secure 9 - 10X worth of that chosen business and make a lot of money.

Sometimes you might have 10X capacity, but about 3X isn't capacity that you want to keep ("C" players, etc.). In that case, you would go find around 6 - 7X worth of business and get rid of the extra capacity.

But what if you have a great team with 10X capacity and there is only 6X of attainable, good quality customers within your chosen focus in your market. In this case, you would still get real good at serving that group of 6X worth of customers. Then you would go find another 4X that is similar to the 6X. This is a better option than leaving 40% of your capacity unused, but will not be as profitable as the PC in the first example.

Back to the "D" cell batteries in Home Depot. It would be more profitable for Home Depot to sell only "D" cell batteries, but not if it causes them to leave 90% of their capacity unused.

To maximize profitability in your Profit Center, you should use most or all of your available capacity to serve a portfolio of high quality customers with very similar needs. If that is not possible, then you must think about how much you want to sacrifice "similar" for the sake of profitability to use up the available capacity that you want to maintain.

The mistake would be to have 10X capacity, fill it with 10-11X of customers, many of which are not in your focus, while good available market within your focus remains un-penetrated. Exacerbating the problem would be to have this scenario plus paying a salesman to attempt to get more business.

Let's get away from the algebra for a minute. The main thing to do is pick a thing to do and get *really, really good* at it so that all the customers of that type that you want to sell to will want to give you all of their business. Whatever you did to get really good may turn out to apply to some other customers that can fill any void in capacity. But be careful. There is only a fine line between taking a little less focused business to fill in the rest of your capacity and having no focus at all.

CAPACITY, CUSTOMER SELECTION, FOCUS AND FOOD

I go to this sports bar down the road from my office. There are two waitresses. The table assignment plan is that whichever waitress greets someone at the door seats them in their section and serves them. All kinds of people from construction workers to lawyers go to this place.

Let me describe the two waitresses. We will call them "smart" and "not-so-smart." Upon the entry of anybody into the establishment, "not-so-smart" (NSS) would be the first one to greet them. She was certainly destined to get the most customers, and all tips are good tips, right? Then there was "smart." She would always have a little trouble getting up out of her chair when that single construction worker came in. While NSS was busy taking his order for a glass of water that she was going to have to refill 8 times, he scoured the menu to decide on the hot dog. His tab of $4.75 would yield a generous $1 tip.

Of course, this left "smart" with nothing to do. But while NSS was refilling water for the hot dog construction worker, the four businessmen come in. At that very moment, I noticed that "smart" had spring in her step after all.

The Air Show

I am at the air show with my boys and notice all the various food venues. The only one that appeared to have any compelling value proposition was the "bratwurst stand." (Think focus here). What they did was grill brats and sell them on a bun for $4. The order processing system was like; "how many", "I'll have two", "that'll be eight bucks." They didn't even serve drinks. Just brats. (Now think capacity and balance). Though they have a 75′ long grill with six guys grilling brats and the order-processing piece only involving nine words, there were about 50 people in line. There was about a 30-minute wait to get your brat. Why? It took no time to serve them. They had tons of cooking power. **But there was only one guy assigned to take the brat, put it on the bun, and put it in the little paper bag thing to serve it in.** This entire time, the servers stood around and waited for him to hand them a brat in a bag. So I stood in line for about 15 minutes then I went and got a hot dog, thinking *Man, they almost had it.*

BY NOW IN THE PROCESS

To somewhat tie these subjects together, it is important to point out that a lot of people should know some things now that they didn't know before. All of your employees, not just office or outside sales, should know the following:

- What market your profit center intends to pursue.
- What makes a customer profitable or not.
- Who are the customers in that chosen market that you want to penetrate further.
- Who are the customers you want to get away from and how to do that.
- What your chosen customers want out of your profit center and what it takes to be the best supplier in the market for those customers.
- What their role is in the process.
- Which vendors you intend to partner with to achieve your stated objectives, and what partnering means (from vendor and distribution side).

Your vendors should know these things:

- What your target market is.

- What value you bring to that market and what value you hope to bring in the future.
- Which customers you are Targeting.
- What you expect from your vendors in your efforts to achieve your objectives.
- What they can expect from you in return.

Your *chosen* customers should know (because they heard it from you, the manager):

- What your target market is and what value you intend to bring to that market.
- That they are one of your chosen customers.
- That you have the ability to change anything that doesn't meet their expectations.

You will find it much easier to achieve your goals if everyone who could help or hurt your efforts knows what it is that you are trying to do. Consider these examples:

Let's say, you have a customer that you really would like to penetrate further. For the purpose of this illustration, let's make him a residential contractor. You are selling him pretty much everything except the loadcenters, which you really would like to convert one day to your brand. The vision of this goal is very clear (in your mind only). Then one day, your gear manufacturer quotes a price for this contractor to your competition just because some punk salesmen asked. Then all the fireworks go off. You call your division manager. You call the gear people etc., etc. I would think that, had your gear guy known that this contractor was a target account for you that he might have made a phone call before quoting the price.

Your inside salesman just received two requests for quote that are each 30 line items long. One is from a cash cow. By the way, in your conversations with this cash cow, he has made it very clear that one thing that is very important to him is that he receives any RFQ that he sends over back as soon as possible. The other RFQ is from one of the least profitable customers you have. Does your inside salesman know which one to do first? Or, is there a 50/50 chance that he might have the cash cow wait until the other quote is done.

Taking it a step further, what if both customers award the order to you. You ship both orders and both customers call with an urgent problem because you shipped the wrong material. Unfortunately, this is holding up work at the jobsite. Your inside salesman should tell the cash cow that he will get the correct parts and get in his personal vehicle to take them out right away. He should tell the other customer that the next truck goes out day after tomorrow, or he is welcome to come to the counter to exchange the parts. Does your inside salesman know to do that?

A final example is you have decided to be the best residential wiring device supplier in town. You just handled an order for one of your target customers very unimpressively. You would hope that the customer would call you and tell you so that you would do better next time. But does that customer know that you desire to be an excellent residential wiring device supplier? If you don't tell him, he just might think that you want to be mediocre.

If everyone who can help you knows what their part is, life will be easy. If they don't know their part, everything is random. Sometimes, when it seems that everyone is working against you, it is just because they don't know what "working for" you means. Lastly, I should point out that it is impossible to communicate anything to anybody until you have decided what it is that you want to do. That is why market focus, customer selection, and customer service are so important.

PUTTING IT ALL TOGETHER

All of the articles so far cover various pieces and parts of running a profit center that are sometimes overlooked. The intention is that each piece should make sense on its own. However, the techniques work best in concert. The purpose of these next few pages is to talk about how to get everything working together to gain a dominant position in your chosen market. To do that, it will be necessary to spend some time on the subject of market analysis and composition but first, let's review what we should know so far:

1. It is very important for PC managers to call on customers, but not just for the sole purpose of selling. More importantly, PC managers should use the competitive advantage they have as CED PC managers to learn what customers need from them so they can tightly weave that input into how they run their profit center.
2. To be highly effective and efficient in serving customers, you are going to have to choose which customer segment that you want to be effective and efficient at serving. Doing any one thing always precludes you from doing something else. It is far more efficient and profitable to do the same thing over and over than to do many different things.

3. Within any given market segment, some customers are going to be more profitable than others. Who those customers are is dependent, among other things, on what you are good at doing. The best way to be really good at serving your highly profitable customers is to stop wasting time with the unprofitable ones.
4. The amount of capacity you have to serve customers is the primary driver of how much you will sell. Since you can't just afford to have tons of everything, you have to be very careful about balancing your capacity so that you have just the right amount of everything. An easy and very expensive mistake you can make is to spend a lot of money on outside sales to ask for more business, when you don't have the capacity to handle more. Also, selling to unprofitable customers significantly reduces your capacity.
5. Customer service has a major impact on the quality of business that you get. Though everyone believes that they provide excellent customer service, too often that service is left up to the individual efforts of certain employees. Not that individual effort is a bad thing but, it can be risky to rely on.
6. There are many reasons that we get business. It is important to understand all of those reasons and make sure that they are properly represented in your profit center. No one or two are always effective and there is

no universally correct mix. Make sure that you don't let yourself get caught in the trap of trying to sell to customers one way when those customers buy another way.

Determining who the customers are and how much they buy

Now, let's take all of this information and position the profit center to effectively penetrate the market in a profitable way. The first thing we need to do is determine the market. It should look something like this:

Kalamazoo Total Electrical Market--$100 million

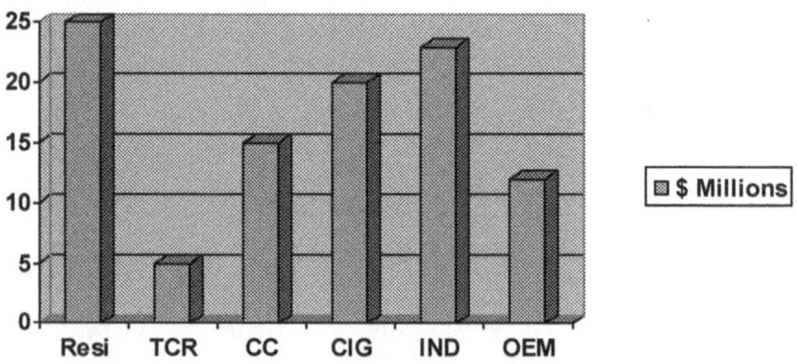

This chart represents the entire $100 mill in the market. Have you ever done an analysis of a market and your first reaction is that there is no way there can be that much available business? There are a couple of reasons why that is the case. In addition to the customers within a given focus that everyone knows about, there are the ones that most don't know exist and the ones that are somewhat tangent to the focus.

"Unknown customers"

On the left-side of the chart is Resi for residential construction. That includes both the resi-contractors that everyone knows about and the ones that no one knows about. This is important because some of the most profitable ones might be the ones that no one knows about because there are fewer competitive threats. A classic example of this is the three man residential electrical contractor that doesn't even put the name of his company on the side of his truck and may not even advertise in the yellow pages. All he does is work on custom homes for one builder. If you are interested in finding these "unknown" customers, there are a number of ways, but the easiest is to capitalize on the opportunity when they call you. "Call me", you say? "How can they call if they are unknown?"

We previously discussed how many customers would switch to a different supplier if they knew there was one out there. Even when they are not looking for a new supplier, they will often have needs that their current supplier can't meet. So they call you. That being the case, you might want to have some kind of strategy in your profit center to capitalize on those **leads** when they come in. If your focus is high-end residential and your inside salesman gets a call for 20- Cat 5 wall plates from someone that you don't normally deal with, that is a lead. He can simply answer the customer's question, or he can capitalize on the opportunity. He can ask questions like, "So what are you doing with these", "Do you use these things often", "What else do you buy", etc.

My favorite story about customers that you don't know about happened just recently. One of our industrial/automation focused profit centers received a call for a 2hp A/C drive from a customer they have never heard of. Of course, the inside salesman does nothing to capitalize on the opportunity, but he does have the sense to pass the message on to the drives specialist. The drives specialist doesn't do anything to capitalize on the opportunity, but he at least passes the somewhat well worn by now message to the PC manager. Who does nothing to capitalize on the opportunity, but does at least give the message to the trainee...who makes a phone call.

Upon asking, the trainee finds out that the customer is a fan OEM that buys thousands of these drives and is looking for a new supplier because of reliability problems. He asks who the decision maker is and finds out that he just moved into town and this is his first day on the job. Poor guy doesn't have a friend in the world. The trainee wrote the business. And what an order it is. The business he locked up is worth over a million dollars per year at nice margins. Here is the best part. This "unknown" customer is right down the street from the profit center!

Tangent focus customers

To the right of RC is TCR. TCR is tangent-commercial-residential. In other words these are customers that are tangent to resi-contractors and tangent to commercial contractors. What I mean by tangent is, though the customer isn't a resi-contractor, his needs are very similar and should be able to be served by a resi-contractor focused distributor. An example of a tangent focus customer comes from a recent profit center visit. The profit center was very clearly focused on residential contractors. The profit center is in the same business park with a company that sells hot tubs. They buy the fiberglass shells and put all the stuff on them and then sell them to retailers. Of course, being a residential contractor house, we don't really get into OEM's like that, but the stuff that they put on those hot tubs includes a 60-amp GFI load center and an A/C disconnect. Particularly considering the proximity to the profit center, this customer could be very profitable. Tangent focus customers aren't in your defined market focus, but their needs match up with your capabilities.

It is important to be aware of the tangent and unknown customers. These customers combined with your known customers make up your entire "customer pool". The larger the "pool", the more selective you can afford to be in selecting those to which you will sell. You want to get a lot of hooks in the water, catch a lot of fish, and then throw some of them back. Remembering the concepts discussed in the customer selection and capacity sections, you should always be looking for ways to refine the profitability of your account portfolio and trading in 2x customers for 1/2x customers. On the other hand, if you have no plan to find out who the rest of the customers in the market are, you won't be able to be selective at all.

Now that you take the tangent focus customers and the unknown customers and add them in with all of the others, you find that that $100 million market is really $100 million after all.

Then there is the market you care about

Now, let's start chopping that $100 million market down to the part that matters to you. Hopefully, you have some kind of focus already, but let's say that you don't. In this example, you at least aren't doing any MRO, or OEM business, so let's lop that off. Now the picture looks like this:

Kalamazoo Modified Market (No MRO & OEM)

$65 Million

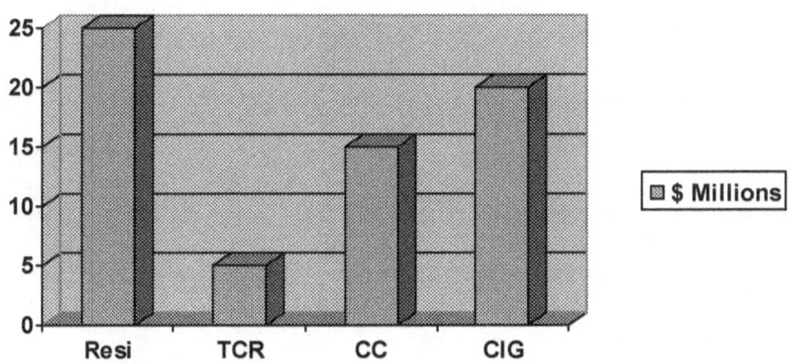

You know that some of the customers within these segments that you currently sell to are unprofitable blood sucking losers (BSL's). So let's trim them off. Now the picture looks like this:

Kalamazoo Further Modified Market (No MRO & OEM & BSL's)

$27 Million

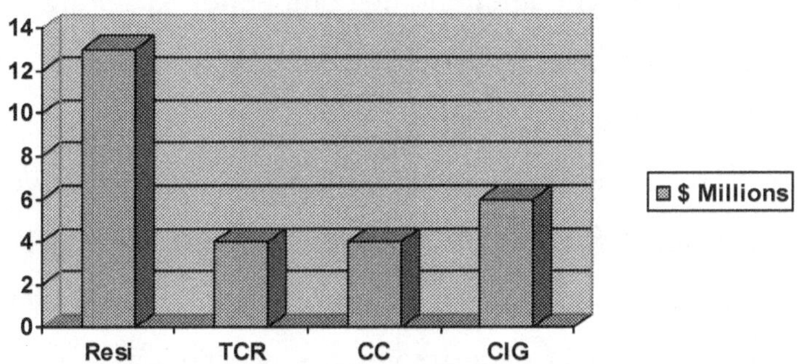

Pick a customer

Notice how each segment has a different percentage of unprofitable customers? This is because your profitability is based upon how good *you* are at servicing any given customer segment. If you are basically a resi-contractor PC that quotes some jobs to those commercial contractors that happen to ask, there will be very few customers within the commercial contractor segment that are profitable to *your PC*.

What is left in the picture is your available market, which is smaller than the original. Your business, on the other hand, is even smaller than that. What you have now is low penetration into a significant part of the market. The trick is to figure out how you can increase penetration in a profitable way.

Here comes another pitch for the concept of market focus. But this time, I am going to approach the subject from a standpoint of building a competitive advantage:

- The better you are than the competition at serving a given customer base, the more battles you will win without using price as a driver.
- By reducing the number of things you try to do you will get far better at doing those things. You get better because you are more focused and many times doing one focused thing precludes you from doing another.

- When you truly become the supplier of choice for a given customer type, your penetration into that customer type will go up dramatically.
- The amount of business that you lose because of becoming more focused will always be less than the amount you gain with your target customers if you choose the proper focus.
- Deeper penetration into a customer is more profitable and is a more defendable position than low penetration.

How to define your focus (the easy way)

At this juncture, you are now going to go through the process of determining what your focus needs to be. Then you will put together a plan to build your profit center so that you can greatly increase your penetration into your chosen market segment.

I was about to type out about a three-page dissertation on the analysis that goes into finding out what market you want to focus on and then how to build your competitive advantage in that market. Then I realized that I was making the entire process way too complex. Here is the simpler version:

- Pick your *favorite customer* that you are doing a pretty good job with and have a pretty good relationship. This customer should be a "CC".

- Find out everything that that customer needs and make sure that you are as good as you can possibly be at doing those things. This should result in your getting all of that customer's business.
- Find another "CC" customer that is like the first one and get their business too.
- Add "CC" customers as you can properly handle them. As you add additional customers, each new one should get easier because your profit center is already built to serve those customers.

Now we will cover these four bullets in a little more detail.

Pick your favorite

Notice that I said to pick your favorite customer. There is a reason that this customer is your favorite. There is some chemistry at work here—some synergy. You have at least some ideas as to what the customer needs and your profit center has the capability of meeting those needs well within their (V/SO). Your goal here is to continue building a competitive advantage around your favorite customer that is difficult if not impossible for your competition to match. This is going to take work. To be successful, the target customer type that you choose must be one that you can get the most passionate about serving. Some people are passionate about lighting jobs with commercial contractors. Some are passionate about pipe and wire. It doesn't really matter, but you aren't going to succeed unless you are trying to become great at something you really want to do.

A side note, if you want to make your job a little easier, you might want to do a check on the customer that you are choosing and see how good the competition is at serving that customer type. So if your favorite customer is large commercial contractors and you are a $2 million profit center in a major market, you might want to think about the battle that lies ahead if you decide to put a whipping on competitors that are thirty times your size and good at what they do. Though I believe that you can get good enough to beat anybody, why not win sooner? It is a lot easier to win with customers that are unknown to the competition than it is to win with the 10 largest contractors in town. In other words, pick the battles that you can win!

Find out what the customer wants

I know, you are thinking, here he goes pointing out the obvious to us again. When I look at what goes on in many profit centers, I see a lot of people thinking that they are asking their customers what they want and giving it to them. But I don't see very many *really* doing it.

The first shortcoming comes in the way we ask the customer what they need. Instead of probing, needs analysis questioning, I see us asking customers questions like, "So, are we treating you

OK?" What is the customer going to say? He is going to respond with something like "fine" so he can go about his business. What I am talking about is really sitting down with the customer and asking him what he wants and needs out of a supplier. This involves things like finding out how the customer runs his business and what that means to a supplier. It means finding out about your customer's customers and how your performance impacts that relationship. Oh, and a little reminder...this is done by the profit center manager—no one else.

In my early days of running a profit center I had a simple conversation with my largest customer. This customer bought $2 million a year in electrical material and we sold about a third of that, making us their largest supplier. Furthermore, my outside salesman had a great relationship with all the key decision makers. As a matter of background, we serviced the customer like this. Everyday, a stack of PO's would come in the mail (yes, this is the old days). Though the PO had a field for "required delivery date", it was blank. An inside sales person would write up the order and send it to the warehouse where it was shipped within the next few days, except for any backorders, which were ordered after the 25th cutoff and subsequently shipped. I was always curious about that blank field on the PO.

Since no one in the profit center could give me an answer about that blank field on the PO, I went to see the storeroom manager and asked him something like, "So, now that I have been here about a year, I was wondering if you could tell me how we are supposed to be processing your orders. I have noticed that the required delivery date field is blank and my people are telling me that that means that the delivery date doesn't matter." The storeroom manager's response went something like this..."Everyday at three P.M., we print out our purchase orders and put them in the mail slot for each supplier. Our good suppliers come by and pick them up. For those that don't, we put them in the mail. My expectation is that the order will be delivered 100% complete the following morning. If by some remote chance there is an unavoidable backorder, I expect to receive a phone call notifying me of that fact and telling me when I should expect the backorder, which should be within 48 hours." At which point, I say, "So what I am hearing is that we aren't doing all that good."

The examples I see in profit centers are not nearly as extreme, but are just as obvious. A classic example is when I go into the profit center and see what the manager is doing. He talks about negotiating price with this vendor, changing wiring device manufacturers (because the salesman never comes by), re-arranging the counter, and looking for that outside salesman so he can grow his business. Then I usually ask something like, "When you talk to customers about what keeps them from buying more from you, what do they say?" The answer usually is "We don't have anything on the shelf, we never have a truck, and we don't get our quotes back on time." We don't have anything on the shelf, so we are going to change wiring device manufacturers. We don't get our quotes back to our customers in time, so we are going to get another outside salesman--Hmmmm.

Really discovering what a customer wants and needs and then providing it is a lot more involved than, "How are we treating you", but, is very easy to do. You need to find out things like this:

- What should you have on the shelf? What should you never run out of?
- When should you open and close the profit center?
- When should you make deliveries? How early? How fast?
- How much technical support do your customers need? Can our people provide that?
- How fast, and in what format, do they want quotes back?
- What brands should you stock?
- Do you need to have any special capabilities like project management and how should that work?
- Does he like the interface with whoever answers the phone?
- Does he like his inside salesperson? Is there a better one out there?
- Does he like his outside salesperson?
- What will it take to get all of his business?

- Try this; **"What can I do to become your #1 supplier?", and "What would it take to get a lot more of your business?**

And the list goes on and on. It does take some skill to come up with all the answers from a given customer. To be successful, I think it is important to recognize some of the barriers. The most common one is pride, as in *your* pride. If you find yourself having a conversation with a customer about what they need, but aren't willing to admit that your profit center has shortcomings; you won't get any serious feedback. Or at least you won't hear it.

Another barrier is that customers just aren't that interested in telling you that you aren't very good at something. This means that you may have to really probe to find out what they need. The last barrier is a little complex. Customers don't know what they need, or how to get it. As an example, a customer may tell you that what he needs is for you to be able to respond to requests for quotes quickly. Is that what he needs? Or could he do his job better if you provided him with a price book with the prices for the products he commonly uses? In other words, don't stop at what the customer says he needs. Keep thinking on how you can make their life easier.

Now do what your customer told you.

Now that you have this list of what the customer really needs, all you have to do is ***do*** those things. Some of you might be thinking that you can't afford any additional capabilities, because you can barely afford what you have now. Remember the *"Capacity"* section and how capacity involves balance and not having more of anything than you need. Take a stroll around your profit center armed with the list that you now have of what the customer needs. Do you have anything that he *didn't* ask for?

Look over there at the counter. A popcorn machine--did he ask for a popcorn machine? Rigid conduit--did he say he needed rigid conduit? The cute counter display of laser levels--does he need laser levels? You will probably see any number of resources that are there, not because your chosen customer wants them there, but because they are just there. I would contend that if you rid yourself of all of those unnecessary resources, you will have plenty of money remaining to spend on what your chosen customers need. Look at it this way, *everything* that you spend money on in your profit center should help provide something that your chosen customer base needs.

Matching your service model (exactly) to your chosen customers

On the subject of what you can afford to provide the customer, it is important to remember that it is easy to give them everything that they really need, as long as you don't get caught up in giving them things that they don't need. You have to have the exact right balance of each component of your service model, for example, say you have a customer that has asked for 30-Advance R2E40S-TP ballasts and 90- Sylvania F40CWSS lamps. You might be thinking that to service that customer, you need to have some lamps and ballasts on the shelf and a way to take orders and deliver them. Here is how different competitors might handle that, depending on their chosen customer base.

1. Supplier #1 has customers that need a relatively competitive price and just need the stuff because they already know what they want. Supplier #1 may also serve many (thousands) of customers so they have to have a low cost position to be able to do that. They will let you place the order, hopefully over the Internet, and ship when their next truck goes that way. Luckily, the customer has a part number, because supplier #1 doesn't do technical support.

2. Supplier #2 is mostly like an electrical distributor. They take the order over the phone and ship what they have. They might, depending on which person takes the order, provide some additional value by asking things like when the customer wants the material delivered.
3. Supplier #3 is an electrical distributor that specializes is lighting and has a core competency in lighting. They will first ask if the customer really wants 90 lamps, since the ballast they are ordering are only two lamp ballasts. They will also ask the customer if they would rather go to the T8 technology, especially since they are replacing the lamps and the ballasts. Of course this supplier puts all of their money into sales and technical expertise, not inventory, so they will have to order all of the material. That is OK, because inventory isn't how they make their customers happy. They will be a little more expensive than suppliers one and two.
4. Supplier #4 doesn't have the product in stock either, but being a lighting showroom, they ask if they can come out and look at the installation to see if their isn't a better fixture to use for the application. They will come up with a great solution, struggle to get the material to the jobsite, and charge an arm and a leg.

The purpose of this example is to show that there are many different ways to handle the same transaction depending on which customers you have chosen to serve and their needs. Supplier #1 will do a good job of serving a maintenance electrician at a hospital who knows what he wants and just needs the material at a good price. Supplier #4 would serve a retail boutique that never deals with things like lighting. Supplier #3 would serve an electrical contractor that does a lot of different things but needs a little help when it comes to the lighting.

If you haven't made that choice, you will either find yourself doing everything (which you can't afford) or nothing. If you haven't made the choice and you try to compete with #1 on price while selling to everybody *and* critically evaluate the bill of material to look for upgrades (which takes time) and go to the jobsite to look at the installation (which takes more time), you will be the greatest supplier on the planet...until next week when you go out of business. If on the other hand, you haven't chosen a customer type and try to do everything all the suppliers do, but do it economically enough to stay in business, you will make every customer you have unhappy and lose them. Remember Gomer.

So remember, your service model has to have exactly the right amount of everything. Not too much and not too little.

Building a competitive advantage

The next part gets a little tricky. It gets tricky because your goal here is to develop a list of competitive advantages that your competition can't match. You have a few already, such as the shear ability to do what you just did. That is to go out to your customers and find out what he needs so you can build your profit center around those needs. Remember, most of your competitors can't do that and the ones who can probably won't. Other competitive advantages that you already have might be people, lines, and your location. What you have to do now is two-fold. First, you will need to *raise the bar* on what the customer needs. Figure out what you can do that is above and beyond what the customer's basic needs are and what he expects. This is a very important point and oddly, one where I see may people doing the opposite. You are now ready to take on a rather challenging and tricky task of developing a list of competitive advantages that your competition can't match.

I was in a profit center once, talking to the manager about a particular customer. The customer called in every day and ordered some material, usually asking for it to be delivered that day. Many times the customer would ask for the material to be delivered within a couple of hours. The customer was a "cash cow" and never asked about the price. The manager was telling me about how he was going to have to have a chat with this customer about his unreasonable requirements and how he needed to plan ahead better. My response to the manager was something like this. "If you have a customer that wants a lift of ½" EMT delivered in an hour, how many competitors do you have?" His answer was one or less. Then I asked, "If that same customer wants the EMT delivered in less than 2 weeks, how many competitors do you have?" The answer there was around 100.

The ideal situation is for your customers to have extremely high requirements that only you can meet. It takes a while, but start thinking about what you can add to your service model that will raise the bar and distance you from the competition.

The next part requires strategic thinking and salesmanship. Through this process, you are building a value proposition that gives you a competitive advantage within your chosen customers. The plan should be that you will have a chosen customer base and a level of penetration that is the envy of the market. It would follow then, that if you are successful at doing that that the entire market is going to try to copy your value proposition and take your business. Now that you have successfully tied the whole process of being able to provide what your customers need, you are going to need to massage what the customers need and your capabilities so that they can't be copied, at least not easily. To do this, you will need to add uniqueness, complexity, and hopefully, *brilliance*. These will give you what we call "barriers to entry."

Uniqueness

Uniqueness means building competitive advantages around things that can't be copied. There are many ways that you can do this, but the two most popular are exclusive lines and people. If you are in the resi-contractor business and you can get all the resi-contractors to want Square D loadcenters and you can get an exclusive on Square D, this is good.

Likewise, people are unique and, of course, some are better than others. If you can build your business around great people that no one else has or can get, that will improve your competitive advantage. Uniqueness only works with things that can't be copied easily. So if you are the only one in your market that opens at 6:00 AM that will only work until it turns out to be a good idea. Then every one else will do it. However, opening at six can help you with complexity.

Complexity

Complexity doesn't mean you have to be complex. It means stringing a number of competitive advantages together to make any attempt at copying them impossible. To use the examples above, if your customers need and you have Square D loadcenters, that great inside salesman, that great counterman, opening at six, and your current location, you will compete handily in your market.

If I was reading this, I would be thinking, "It sure seems a lot easier to get Square D and open at six than it does to do all that hard stuff like finding out what my customers want and building my business around that. I think I will skip all the hard stuff." And I would be wrong. The rules of this capitalist society deem that the customers are eventually going to get what they want. A classic example of this is the supplier that has the exclusive line that gives his customers no choice but to buy from him. He proceeds to just milk all the profit he can out of the line and his customers while providing mediocre service. The competitor down the street builds a better service model for those customers and starts to make inroads into some of the non-specified commodity business. Then, one day, WHAM! He gets your exclusive line.

Brilliance

Just about anybody can increase and decrease the ingredients that make up their service model and competitive advantage. Sure, complexity makes it harder for others to copy you, but it is still possible. If you want to really throw a monkey wrench into the competition's plans, hit them with some brilliance. Brilliance is being better than your competition at finding out what your chosen customer base needs and coming up with better solutions to meet those needs. An example of brilliance is a distributor in a high traffic congested market that decides to, instead of fighting traffic all day long to get stuff to the customers late, comes up with the idea of putting job lock boxes on the jobsites of his contractors and then delivers to them at night. He cuts his cost relative to the competition, and his customers have their material as soon as they come to work in the morning.

Actually, this brilliance subject points again to the competitive dynamics of focus. I am pretty sure that the distributor manager that thought of the night delivery idea doesn't think obsessively about how to serve eight different customer types better while he is taking shower in the morning.

At this point in the journey, you have found a customer type that you like and that is a good fit for your profit center. You have found out what those customers need and given it to them. You have then raised the bar on those customer expectations and made your competitive advantage one that has plenty of barriers to entry like people, exclusive lines, brilliance and complexity. You are almost done. There are only a couple of things left to do. First, tell everybody. And second, go find some more of these customers.

Tell everybody

Your employees and your suppliers and for that matter, other customers need to know who your chosen customers are and what it is that you provide them and why. Hopefully at this point you have some sort of a vision about whom you want to sell to and what you need to do for that customer. But we don't make profit in our mind. Everyone in the profit center has to be executing the same vision as you.

Is this the hard way or easy way?

I would expect that many people would read this and think that all this stuff is way too hard. You just want to go back to the simple life that you were leading before. Of course you can do that, though I would argue that what is discussed here is a lot simpler than what most people in electrical distribution do (which is work their tails off trying to serve many different masters). But if you don't want to do these things, you can still help yourself. *Just think about everything above and try not to do the opposite.* So when a customer offers a piece of constructive criticism, don't argue with him. When you see a customer raising the bar on their requirements from you with things that you can do, don't discourage it. When a customer that has entirely different needs than the (cash cow) customers asks you to change what you do (usually through the input from a poorly directed, commissioned outside salesman), don't do it.

And, lastly, get some more customers just like the first one.

Now that you have built your service model with all the appropriate competitive advantages and barriers to entry, you can plow your way through the market like a hot steak knife through butter. Every customer that you now pursue will need nothing other than what you are already doing. Your sales pitch will be impossible to say no to. It will go like this, "Of all the customers in the market, we only cater to ones like you. If guys like you need it, we do it. If guys like you don't need it, we don't do it. If we don't do it yet and you need it, then we will start. Where our competitors spend their day trying to make a lot of customers that aren't like you happy, our entire passion in life is to get better and better at serving customers like you."

I know that in real life, things might not be quite that simple. You might be thinking that there just aren't that many similar customers in your market. Remember that there are customers that you don't know about yet and tangent focus customers that you might not have thought about. Once you have a focus that you want to get great at, you will need to have a plan to seek out the customers that fit your capabilities.

Another point to remember is that your focus does not need to be an exact customer type. It just has to be *something* that you have chosen to do. Maybe you choose to sell fuses to those that need fuses. Maybe you want to be the guy that has everything on the shelf. Maybe you want to be the fast guy. Maybe you want to be the gear guy. Etc.

As you embark on finding these new customers to sell your unbeatable service model to, every new one will involve some decisions. They aren't going to be exactly like the other ones and may require that you modify your service model somewhat. If the modification requires that you raise the bar on what you do, that can be good. On the other hand, if the modification requires that you change something that conflicts with what you are doing with your other customers that is a slippery slope that you don't want to get on. It really requires discipline to be good over the long haul.

The competitive landscape

Everything that you do now can be written down as your competitive capabilities. Along with those capabilities there are things that could determine your chances of success with a given customer, i.e., the competitive landscape. For any given customer opportunity, you could score them based on whether they need each of your competitive capabilities and whether you would have to modify or expand your capabilities. You could also do the same thing for the incumbent supplier. If the customer needs more of your capabilities and less of the competition's it *ought* to be your customer, so go take what is rightfully yours. If the customer needs many of your capabilities, but will require that you add an additional capability, such as delivering material at 6:00 AM, it could also be a viable target, though you will have to evaluate the profitability of the account based on the expense of the additional service offerings. If, on the other hand, the customer needs few of your capabilities, and more of the competition's capabilities, the customer is not rightfully yours to take, so don't waste your time and resources.

Do you only get the business that is rightfully yours?

I make it sound like that, based on the capabilities that you have compared to the competition, somebody is destined to lose before the battle begins. Some people would compare that with their own experience where they have pursued all kinds of business that wasn't "rightfully theirs to take", and gotten orders. There are many reasons that this happens, most of which are discussed in *"Sales Strategy Mistakes."* Interestingly, most of the ways that you can get business that you don't deserve are not profitable over the long haul. As an example, let's say that you are a pretty good custom home residential distributor. You have an outside salesman that calls on a large, commercial contractor. Of course this isn't your bailiwick, but you get some business anyway. Here are the unprofitable ways that you are getting this business:

- Price—sometimes you quote things at levels your competition just doesn't want to get to.
- The customer needs you as a quote service to keep their preferred distributor honest so they give you one out of ten orders to keep you providing that service.
- There are orders that the preferred distributor just doesn't want.
- Random matching of your inventory to their needs on an occasional basis when the preferred supplier doesn't have something in stock.
- Pity—most customers will give a salesman at least a few crumbs every now and then just because they feel sorry for them.

If I were a large contractor focused distributor that planned to be the best in town some day, selling to this customer under these circumstances would be OK. I would be willing to take my licks to prove myself and even these sorry reasons for getting orders would be great ways to do just that. Of course, I would be aware that until

I get into a more dominant position, I will probably be losing money.

If, on the other hand, I was the custom-resi distributor described above, I would run from this business as fast as I could. The quoting activity would just suck up valuable resources for unprofitable orders. The orders that I did get wouldn't be good ones and they would also suck up resources that could be used to make progress with my good customers. Even the random use of my inventory would be inefficient and unprofitable. Though I stock many residential wiring devices, the commercial contractor will occasionally buy commercial devices. Now I find my self starting to stock some commercial devices. This leads me to never have enough, until inventory time when I have too many and they go on writedown. Everything that I do to serve this customer causes me to lose money and use up valuable resources.

What about the customers that you already have?

What about all your other existing customers? You have picked a certain set of customers and built a supply house around them, which should be a very profitable endeavor. Do you just fire the other 80% of your customers? Of course not, you just stop catering to their needs. Everything you do for them will come after what you do for your target customers. Over time, the ones that need to go away will go away. As you become more and more successful at pursuing your target customers, you will have less and less time to deal with the customers that are not part of your focus. The classic example of this is the profit center manager that is complaining about the little old ladies that come into the profit center and spend an hour picking out one candelabra light bulb. My advice to that manager is that the problem is not that the little old lady came in, but that she didn't see five contractors in front of her in line, each with a 20 item bill of material. If she saw that, she would leave.

PUTTING IT ALL TOGETHER WITH OUTSIDE SALES

Putting it all together..." has a notable lack of mention of anything having to do with the outside sales function. That lack of mention is for a reason which is that this entire subject must to be yours (the Profit Center Manager's) to deal with. You don't want each outside salesman developing his own vision and building his own mini-supply house around his favorite customer type. It just doesn't work. Actually, when you look at most profit centers with outside salesmen (particularly if they are on commission) you will see some element of them running their own business with their own focus.

Driving the process of attacking the market is your primary charge, but account assignments do play a vital role in the process so I will cover that here.

First we have to break down the simple subject of finding a customer and getting all of his business. There are three stages of relationships that you have with a customer that you are trying to penetrate.

- Getting your foot in the door. This is normally an unprofitable position, but you have to do it to get any further.
- Nurturing and growing the relationship to get in a strong position (possibly a strong number two).
- Becoming the dominant supplier.

Depending on the size of the customer and the resources you are able to devote to it, getting through the three bullets could take months or even years.

Now for the account assignments

Within a given salesman's account package, there is probably one account that is "rightfully yours", meaning that that customer's needs match up very well with the profit center's capabilities. The ideal situation would be for you to personally go get that business. But let's say that you already have another account that you are pursuing and you want to delegate responsibility for cracking this account to your outside salesman. Now that you have chosen the first, ideal account for him to pursue, *you have a decision to make.* **How much do you want to reduce that outside salesman's effort in making real progress at the account?** By half? Then give him one more account. By 90%? Then give him nine more accounts. In my travels, I have seen two distinctly different types of profit centers. The ones that tend to grow profitably usually make real account penetration progress at one or two accounts per year. The ones that don't grow are usually not in the dominant position with many accounts and are trying to "magically" move to a dominant position with 50 accounts at a time.

With every account within your focus, in a given year you should be trying to do one of the following:

- Get your foot in the door.
- Move from getting your foot in the door to gaining a significant position in preparation for the "kill."
- Move into a dominant position.
- Maintain after moving into a dominant position.
- Do nothing—Status Quo.

Each salesman should then have a certain mix of each of these types of accounts. That mix could be different depending on the salesman. You might have a salesman who is a good farmer that can maintain well while you provide the services of "cracking" the account, as an example, but don't go overboard on the idea of the outside salesman providing a maintenance service, remember that the assumption that we usually need an outside sales person to maintain an account is just that, an *assumption.* Inside sales and the counter function can do a fine job of maintaining certain accounts. That can be important to remember when you are trying to determine how to properly deploy your outside sales force to make the most progress with the accounts that you choose to pursue.

To Summarize:

1. As discussed in "Putting it all Together", *you* need to develop *your* strategy to attack the market.
2. Use *your* field sales force along with your own talents to win what you need to win.
3. Remember that there are steps in the evolution of the customer relationship.
4. Just like a P.C., the less things an outside salesman tries to accomplish, the more effective he will be.

"Man who chases two rabbits has no meat for dinner"

Chinese Proverb

PROFIT SHARING AS A COMPETITIVE ADVANTAGE

I was talking to my biggest customer one time, (this is the same one that I found out we had been handling his orders wrong the whole time), and asked him what I would have to do to deserve more of his business. Rather than answer my question, (I should have known it wouldn't be that easy), he responded by asking me, "why would I want to give you business any more than one of your competitors?" I said,

> you know, that is a good question...There are two primary reasons. First of all, *I am in charge*. I don't mean that I am anything special, but that I ***run*** our Profit Center. The people that run my competition's place are in far removed places like St. Louis. Have you ever met them? You are sitting in front of me right now and can tell me anything you want me to do and, if I decide it is a good idea, I will go do it; if you ever have a problem, tell me and I will fix it.
>
> I continued, The second is the big one. I don't know, but I would suspect that, with just about any supply house that calls on you, the salesmen is interested in your business. He is paid on commission. His boss, the

> manager, is probably paid some kind of performance bonus also, and cares about your business as a result. I suspect that everyone else in the branch just wants to keep their job. Everyone in my profit center is paid profit sharing based on our location's performance. And it is a significant part of their income. Whether we keep your business or not means thousands of dollars in personal income to my truck driver. When you call our profit center and Louise answers the phone and treats you so cordially, always remembering your name...it is because she wants to keep your business so she can get her kids new shoes for school.

You are going to think I am making this up. Not two weeks after this conversation, we delivered a bunch of special ordered 20′ bussbar to this customer in a wooden crate. They needed it badly. Unfortunately, one of their employees just thought it was a crate and threw the crate in a dumpster, which promptly got carried off to the landfill. Later that day, our truck driver, Raymond was back out at the customer making another delivery and learned of the buss bar fiasco. The customer was in a big bind now. You know what Raymond did? He went to the dump and looked till he found the buss bar.

THE INEVITABLE PUSHBACK

I was discussing this subject at a recent meeting of PC Managers and, after a while, a couple of them basically said that it just isn't that simple in their profit centers. To describe their situation, both of the profit centers were pursuing a given market (in this case the industrial market), yet did quite a bit of business in another market (commercial and residential contractors). In one case, it was because the market was quite small and the PC Manager didn't feel that he could be very selective and in the other case, though the manager put most of his effort in the industrial market, his contractor business was growing faster. Both managers asked if the topics we had been discussing meant that they should abandon all of that business.

I probed a little deeper into the subject of their penetration into the industrial business. As is almost always the case, both PC's lost a considerable amount of business in their primary focus area to other distributors. The PC in the larger market had a competitor that was generally better than he was at the industrial business. The other PC was in a very small market and was the only distributor in that market, yet he still managed to lose quite a bit of business to a couple of industrial distributors from 100 miles away, including the largest industrial customer in the market. My first observation was that this was exactly according to plan. I have yet to see a distributor pursue multiple markets and dominate either one. (That is not to say that it never happens, I just haven't seen it).

Life lessons in Focus

In thinking about how to clarify the subject of customer selection and market focus as it relates to market dominance and profitability, I thought of an analogy. I am not a big NASCAR fan, but I do have somewhat of an understanding of how the cars work. That understanding comes from a familiar knowledge base called a Sony Playstation 2. When you tune a NASCAR car, there are a number of adjustments that make it work best on the track that it is going to race on. One of the adjustments is an airfoil thing on the back of the car-- it might be called a spoiler. This spoiler can be set at a high angle (tilted up a lot in the back), or a relatively flat angle. With a high angle, the car is pushed down more from the wind and gets better traction. But it goes slower. At a relatively flat angle, the car goes faster, but has less traction. With the Sony Playstation 2, there are these little bar graphs that go up and down as you adjust the rear spoiler to help you figure out how you want to fine-tune it. Turn it one way and the speed graph goes up and the traction graph goes down. Turn it the other way and the opposite happens. Obviously, one wouldn't conclude that spoilers are good or bad, or that they should universally be set at a high angle or flat. It depends on the situation and whether you need speed or traction. So when I am racing at Bristol on the Playstation, I put the spoiler at a high angle. At Daytona, I put a low angle. (Then I proceed to wreck the car about every 5 seconds.)

If Sony had an electrical distribution Playstation game, it would have the same little bar graphs, just with different names. If you increase focus, you will be a better competitor relative to your competition and, as a result, your market penetration will go up. Depending on your competitors you might need a lot of focus to be able to compete better. This is most often the case in a larger market. If you are in a smaller market, with weaker competitors, you might not need to be such a great competitor, so you might not need as much focus. You can go after a few more things, knowing that you won't be as good at any of them, but thinking that you will be competitive enough because of the lack of competition.

Just as the market penetration graph goes up with the focus graph, the available market bar graph goes down. In a large market, I wouldn't be that worried about that because there is plenty of available market. I just need to be able to win battles profitably. In a very small market, I would think a little longer before I eliminated from my target market any major chunks of the market. And that would be OK, because I wouldn't have to be as good.

I should point out that larger and smaller are relative. You can be in a quite small market and have only one segment provide all the business you need. In the case of the smaller market Profit Center from the meeting, he was in a very small market and was doing about $1 million a year in sales to many market segments.

Interestingly, that same small market had about $5 million in available industrial business that he wasn't getting.

So, just as I give you that "it's a small market, so I don't have to be all that focused" excuse, I take it away.

I should also point out that, though there is that relationship between focus, penetration, and available market that would require different decisions be made in different markets, the profitability subject is a relative constant. In other words, no matter what market you are in, as long as there is enough available business to cover your rent, the more focused you are the more profitable you can be. The same holds true with customer selection. The more selective you are, the more profitable you will be.

In closing, just remember that all of the previously discussed topics, including customer service, capacity, focus, selection, etc. impact the "bar graphs" and are related. And none of them are switches that you turn on or off. They are matters of degree and at any point in time one of them needs to be tuned a little differently to, hopefully, win the race.

APPENDIX #1: THOUGHTS ON PRICING

As you may recall, the basic thesis of "the articles" is that these are things that you need to know, but may not be typically taught. The primary focus of the main body of the articles is around the proper way to attack a market. You will notice that it specifically talks a lot about the laws and theories that apply to how an electrical distributor should position itself in a market and specifically doesn't tell anyone exactly what to do. That is primarily because the various subjects are far too complex and interwoven for anyone other than the profit center manager himself to decide what to do at any moment.

These two factors have led to the need for an appendix, and what you are now reading is the maiden article in the appendix. The appendices:

- Probably won't deal with how to attack a market or place oneself in a market in any sort of specific fashion.
- Could include articles that have nothing to do with attacking a market.
- May or may not be specific, depending on what I decide at the time.

- Won't necessarily be distributed with the rest of "the articles."
- Are similar to "the articles" in that, if you don't like one of them, the rest are free.

So, on to pricing. Remember the thesis of these articles is to discuss what isn't typically discussed. That being the case, I won't be redundant and say things like "all things being equal, if one guy has a higher stock GP than another, he will make a lot more money." I want to talk about the rest of it.

As I was thinking about pricing this morning, a few experiences of mine from the past year or two came to mind. Let me first tell these six quick stories, and then let's see if they provide any lessons when looked at together.

Story #1. I am on a plane flying to one of our supplier's advisory council meeting. On the way there I am sitting next to this lady that is working on a massive project for the company she works for--Dollar General. This massive project includes a 4" thick binder full of research in addition to what is in her laptop computer. She has assembled a team of others throughout the country to help her come up with the right ideas and to beta test them. Her research includes every kind of statistical analysis you could think of to evaluate sales, gross profit, and net profit, based on execution of all of the various possible scenarios. The results of her project will determine whether she gets her five figure performance bonus at the end of the year, so she is desperate to make sure that she succeeds.

Here is the project: *Determine what will provide the most bottom line profit for the company; selling an 8oz. can of chili beans for 35 cents each, or three for a dollar.*

Story #2. I land in Orlando for the advisory council meeting. We break out into various problem solving teams to come up with solutions to this vexing problem: *How do we deal with that long term inside salesman who just puts cost plus 15 on everything?*

Story #3. I am at an ethics in leadership seminar and am having discussions with my breakout partner who manages a number of product managers for Mac Tools. For those of you that don't know, Mac Tools is a high end tool company that sells tools to work on cars and things like that, (or "things of that nature" as Schwarzenegger would say). Their primary customer audience is race car mechanics. So selling to them is like selling to an electrical contractor. In other words, they aren't just average Joe consumer. I ask my partner what a "product manager" does. He tells me "it is all about mix. What a good product manager does is determine what tool they can run a special on at a NASCAR race that will get the mechanics to come to their display truck. They then predict how many of those products they will sell at a 25% loss and make sure that they have enough other, highly intriguing products appropriately priced to make up the losses and earn enough profit on top of that to make the margin that the company needs to make." I respond with something like "yeah, I know what you are talking about. We do something like that, just not *exactly."*

Story #4. There is a profit center that is chronically losing money to the point that they have made it onto the special "loss house turnaround" list. This means that doing something different would probably be a really good idea and that all of us in management are willing to offer all of the advice that we can think of to help. It is suggested that the profit center is in a market situation that should allow it to charge significantly more on its out of stock sales. The profit center Manager agrees with that suggestion. The only problem is that his largest customer, which is a significant fraction of his business, is an industrial user that has quite low margins and hasn't historically been conducive to prices increases. After an extensive evaluation of the profitability of that customer, for some reason, the manager, possibly out of desperation, develops such a resolve to raise his margins that he goes to that major industrial and tells him that he needs to raise his margins by 11 points, or he isn't going to sell to him any longer! The customer responds by saying that if that is what it takes to keep him as a supplier, then that is what it takes, so up the prices go. That profit center was losing money at the time and now will at least be in the second quartile at the time of this writing, if not the first.

Story #5. I go to Dillards department store shortly after Christmas to do my annual clothes shopping. The people in the men's section are working harder than they did during Christmas, even though I am the only one there. I listen to them talking and determine that they have pricing specialists that are watching sales of every item and marking them down by the hour. Their goal is to sell as many as possible at 30% off before going to 40% off, then to sell as many at 40% off before going to 50% off. It reminds me of something that should be happening on the NYSE.

Story #6. I am having a discussion with a manager of a profit center that is selling to a customer that is clearly in a neighboring profit center's back yard. Due to the capabilities of the two profit centers and their proximity, this seemed a little odd to me, so I asked the profit center why that was. His answer was "that customer isn't real big--only buys about $100k per year. About five years ago he went into that profit center and bought a $3 bell box (or single-gang weatherproof box, depending on which language you speak). Only problem was, they charged him $9. He didn't complain, he just determined that he was never going back there again, because he knew he couldn't trust that profit center." His story made me think of those times when someone has said something like, "we raised our margins 7% to this customer class and almost no one complained."

Put all of these stories together and what conclusions do you draw? I probably should close this thing out right here and let you just contemplate that answer. But I can't resist offering a few observations:

- We as an industry are somewhere between simplistic and ignorant when it comes to pricing.
- Though for most profit centers, it wouldn't be prudent to create any new positions like "pricing manager", it is important to remember that there is a lot more work to be done to have optimized pricing than most realize.
- For everything that is sold to a particular customer there is a "perfect" price. That perfect price will have the right combination of profit maximization, consistency, market penetration (which you might want to be high or low, depending on who the customer is), and *trust.*
- You can't decide what your pricing strategy should be until after you decide what your place in the market will be (your focus, value, etc.). In fact, your pricing strategy doesn't support your place in the market; it in part *defines* your place in the market.
- Taking the three previous bullets together, if you currently spend 98% of your time selling and 2% pricing, shifting about 6-8% more towards pricing would probably be smart. In fact, you could just find some

unprofitable customers to fire and use that spare time on the pricing piece.

- Remember that spending time with pricing doesn't just involve sitting at your desk and "tweaking." That is the implementation of the pricing. The bigger part is finding out what the right price should be. Remember the Dollar General chili bean lady.
- If you sell any significant amount of non-stock material, that subject deserves as much attention as the price matrix does.

Remember that you don't sell things just to make money. If you did, everything would be easy. I can think of a few reasons to sell things. One is to get some run time with a customer to prove to him that you are worthy of being a bigger supplier to him than you have been in the past. Another, might be because one of your suppliers really needs that volume. Another is that *you* need that volume to help inventory flow and to be able to buy at the right price. This is discussed in greater detail in the article on "Customer Selection." And of course, there is the tactic of the "Mac Tool" product manager, who sells one thing really cheap to get a customer in the door, so that that customer will buy something else at a higher margin.

Hopefully, this article has once again continued the tradition of exploring the subject at hand and providing greater insight, provoking thought, while giving no real answers at all. That is for you to do.

APPENDIX #2: VENDOR RELATIONS

(Like everything else in life, you get what you deserve!)

The thesis statement that I will attempt to defend is this: Vendors usually treat you exactly as you should be treated.

You are thinking "Yeah, but what about the unmotivated and unintelligent ones like the ones that call on me?" Well, you are right, in part. Manufacturers and reps are no different than us. They can be just as prone as we are to allow a salesman that is paid on straight commission to have a nice juicy territory that allows him to not call on many of his accounts and still make a good living. They can even be guilty of not following up with that salesman on specific objectives, or not ensure that he has a plan. They can also allow a salesman that just plain doesn't get it done to remain in the job. But can we criticize them for doing what we do? Getting back to the thesis statement:

A) Here is what you should expect from a vendor:

- Pricing that keeps you as competitive as you need to be
- Sales support as you deem necessary
- Favor over the competition where it is appropriate

- An interest in your business
- Help with inventory support, promotions, or joint calls, etc.
- Active participation in your ongoing sales strategy in the market
- A strategy of exclusivity with regard to distribution that is consistent with the product
- Information on market intelligence such as what the competitors are doing or who the underpaid/available talent is within the competition

I would guess that you might be thinking that is a pretty high bar. I don't think it is. You just usually don't see that kind of behavior because you don't inform the vendors of your expectations, or you don't deserve such behavior.

B) In return for the above, here is what you should provide a vendor:

- Adequate inventory support to make sure that his product is well represented physically in the market
- Sales support to ensure that his product is not only sold, but preferred by the predominance of your target customers

- Appropriate training of your people on the vendor's products
- A clearly articulated market strategy that defines your place in the market and, as a result, defines your value to the supplier
- An ongoing sales strategy that will result in increased sales for that supplier
- A value proposition to go along with that market strategy that is clearly articulated
- An operational interface that is relatively low cost to the vendor, i.e., not asking for returns of silly items (you know, the $10 part that you have sold 20 in the last year, but still have 3 on writedown)
- A level of exclusivity that is consistent with the product
- Ultimately, you should provide a vendor with market share that meets that vendor's goals

What I would recommend that you take from these two little sections is that:

a) You should expect all of these things from your suppliers and,

b) You should make sure that you are doing your part in return.

If you find yourself lacking in a), then you should evaluate your b). Ask yourself these kinds of questions:

- If I were a supplier, would I want to come to this profit center to make my sales calls? Am I welcome? Will this profit center take me (monetarily) where I want to go?
- How much am I worth to this supplier? Do I purchase enough product to matter, and am I exclusive enough? Do I control the market, or do I feed off of other's efforts?
- Does my supplier know what my place is in the market and how that place is going to help him? Have I asked my supplier what he needs or expects from me?

I think that the confusion some of us get into is that we get bogged down into thinking that our suppliers need us, as though the business wouldn't exist without us—like we are the customer or something.

I am currently remodeling my kitchen (or at least, my wife is) and I am sure that the business (and the resulting noticeable rise in the nation's GDP) would not exist if we didn't do the remodeling project. But that is not what we distributors generally do. All we do is *involve* ourselves in business that is going to happen anyway.

My favorite memory of this sort of confusion is when a PC Manager, who was about to get cut off by GE-Gear (and let me tell you, that is hard to do), complained about the service she was getting and lamented "I spend $200,000 a year with these people; they had better give me some attention." I don't know, but I am thinking that no one called the CEO on his cell phone to report that statement.

Before closing this thing out, let me tell you another story. When I ran a profit center, I was in the industrial market and we sold Class I, Div II lighting fixtures. Those were our "layins." About a third of the projects were spec'd Crouse Hinds, which I sold, as did two other distributors. The rest of the business was either controlled by another manufacturer, or Crouse couldn't get competitive. As a result, our profit center, like the other two Crouse distributors in town had a couple of other lines to get the rest of the business. I was in the fortunate position of never having provided any value to any of the manufacturers so I didn't have any great ties. So I cut off everyone except Crouse. When Crouse lost the order, I lost the order—but I lost it trying to the end, as did Crouse.

So what happened? Well my share of the orders that went Crouse went from about a third to around 90%. Crouse knew that I was on their team and always supported me. Crouse was unsure about the other two guys. Crouse and I found out that by sticking with each other, we could get about half of those orders as well, because it wasn't as hard to convert the business as we thought after all. And the orders that I wrote, Crouse made sure that I made plenty of profit. Even when that wasn't possible, Crouse made sure that I made more money somewhere else. Things became a lot more profitable when Crouse and I decided to work for a cause and not just quote whatever came our way.

That brings me to two of the lessons of vendor relations:

- First, single line is almost always better.
- And second, if you can't be single line, let each supplier know where they stand. Let him know what business he can expect to get and what business he shouldn't expect to get.

Put yourself in the supplier's shoes for a minute (or always). Where do you put the support? With the guy who always sells your product, or the one who sometimes sells your product? Even if you have to choose between those who only sometimes sell your product, will you more often support the one who you know when you are in or out or the one where you don't know until you have won or lost an order? Would you support the bigger guy or the little guy? Would you support the one who has a plan, or the one who doesn't?

I will tell you yet another story. I used to have a salesman that used one of my least favorite phrases. He would say "that is a nice quote." Back in my old days, when I wasn't *nearly* as polished and professional as I am now, I would respond with "Are we going to get that order?" At which point, he would say—it depends on if we are low. I would then throw the quote in the trash and tell him, "When you have one you know we are going to get, let me know. We will quote that one." Granted, there might have been smoother ways to handle that, but I will stick with my point.

On any given piece of business, someone has done the work to bring it to the point of a quote. If it is you, that's good. If not, then you are playing the role of the leach. There are two things to consider when playing the role of the leach. First, don't expect a fair shake. You haven't done the work. And second, if you demand a fair shake, not only will you not write a profitable order, you will be in a lot worse position with the vendor than if you had never been involved in the first place.

To state it differently, taking orders, but not selling the customer provides virtually no value to a supplier. Taking orders when another distributor has done the selling actually reduces value to the supplier because it causes friction between the supplier and the distributor that is doing the work. For more insight on avoiding being a leach, look at the other sections in the book, (market focus, customer service, sales strategy mistakes).

I would expect that many readers might look at the previous sections and compare them to the reality that they are currently experiencing in their profit center and think, "That all looks good on paper, but I have all kinds of exceptions that just don't allow things to work that way in my profit center." I would bet that if you ran your profit center through all the filters of all the other subjects in the book, you will see that those exceptions are either imagined, or caused by your own profit center's actions. For example:

- Your outside salesman tells you that you need to carry both line A and line B. Go ask the customer yourself and you might get a different story. Or you might find out that if you "sell" instead of just taking orders, you won't need both lines.
- A vendor rarely supports you on job quotes. Look at who is doing all the work up front. Consider whether you are even perceived to be a player in that market by your customers. Is it possible that the vendor thinks that you are supporting your other supplier?
- A particular supplier "never comes by." Does he know why he should? Is there anything going on? Or is he just going to get another request for return?

As distributors, we charge a profit. That profit should be roughly equivalent to the amount of value we provide. The more things we do, the more value we provide and therefore, the more profit we make, and visa versa. Using that thought process the most profitable business would be where the distributor determines what the customer needs and creates a product to meet that need. The distributor then has a manufacturer make a few truckloads of the product especially for the distributor who then warehouses the product and sells it to the customer. In this scenario, the distributor would determine the buy price and the sell price, and if he has any sense, there would be a sizable spread between the two!

The opposite scenario would be where the manufacturer determines the customer's needs and creates a product for those needs. The manufacturer then markets the product to the customer and provides any sales support that is needed, i.e., take-offs, specification work, expediting, etc. The manufacturer then ships directly to the customer so no warehousing is needed and the distributor processes a direct payable and collects the money. An astute reader would notice that I just described the current state of the contractor lighting business in many markets in the U.S. And you know who sets the buy and sell price in this scenario don't you? Ever had a lighting rep come to you and say something like, "I just wrote this $100k lighting job and I want you to handle the billing...I have 35% percent in it for you, is that enough?"

The power (and margin) goes with the one who provides the value. In other words, you get what you deserve. Think about the previous point and think about how often we shoot ourselves in the foot. The lighting business is what it is because we distributors eagerly allowed all of the value to shift from the distributor to the lighting reps. Now we don't like the fact that millions of dollars of profit no longer exist in the electrical distribution channel. The opposite trend is occurring today with most gear manufacturers. The manufacturers are asking distributors to take on more and more of the quotation work and provide more and more of the value in the process. So why do we complain? We shouldn't! My opinion is that this is one heck of an opportunity for distributors to put more money in their pocket. Now, when we see a way to reconfigure a gear layout that is more cost effective, we can pocket the money, not the manufacturer.

If you read the section on sales strategy mistakes, you might have been thinking how in the world that section made it through the editing process without being culled. I hope that now that you are reading this section, it makes more sense. Think about this. Many of us often get confused into thinking that it is normal for us to have business where we provide virtually no value, yet still make a hefty profit. I would contend that that is business that goes under a category of business that you have because "you haven't lost it yet", or because "you were there." Those things can happen. But don't think that it is the way things will continue. Consider yourself lucky. The capitalist society in which we live deems that anyone that is getting more than they deserve won't get it for long.

A few more miscellaneous points

- Remember that it is vendor *relations.* Whatever you do, it will work better if you first develop a relationship with the supplier. They are people just like you that are just trying to do a job. Get to know them. Learn what is important in their life. Though I believe all of the above dynamics hold true, it is also true that you can get a little more than you deserve if you first develop a strong relationship foundation with your supplier.

- In general, you are better off if you change lines less. You should only change lines when you have done everything to support your end of the bargain and the supplier just doesn't get it. The grass is rarely greener on the other side. If you are forced to change lines, you should honestly tell your supplier why you are doing so. As a matter of fact, you should do so before you get to the decision to change lines. Give vendors every opportunity to mend their ways.
- You should always be honest with your vendors. If you want a better price on a job so you can make more money, then you should say just that. Making up some kind of story about a competitive threat that doesn't exist will work maybe once. The suppliers will almost always find out the truth, which will harm your relationship in the long run. Besides, telling the truth is always the ethical thing to do.

As you look at the state of your profit center. Remember that your suppliers can act like grease, or they can act like brakes. They can make everything easier, or a lot harder. They will respond in a manner to give you what you probably deserve.

www.ingramcontent.com/pod-product-compliance
Lightning Source LLC
LaVergne TN
LVHW041215150826
845673LV00001B/415

* 9 7 8 0 9 7 6 4 9 4 0 9 6 *